# *The* Birds

## *of* Pandemonium

### *Life Among the Exotic and the Endangered*

MICHELE RAFFIN

ALGONQUIN BOOKS OF CHAPEL HILL    2014

Published by
ALGONQUIN BOOKS OF CHAPEL HILL
Post Office Box 2225
Chapel Hill, North Carolina 27515-2225

a division of
WORKMAN PUBLISHING
225 Varick Street
New York, New York 10014

Library of Congress Cataloging-in-Publication Control Number: 2014023612
ISBN 978-1-61620-136-4

10 9 8 7 6 5 4 3 2 1
First Edition

Pandemonium Aviaries
PO Box 240
Los Altos, CA 94024
www.PandemoniumAviaries.org

For Nick, Jason, Ross, and Lizzy

# Contents

# The Tao of Oscar, Architect Finch

I'm a sucker for free stuff, so when a friend told me about a big birdcage sitting by the side of the road with a sign tied to it that read FREE AVIARY, FREE BIRD, INQUIRE WITHIN, I hustled right over to have a look. I was just starting out on the avian adventure that inspired this book, and any added cage space was welcome. I didn't need another bird for our backyard sanctuary at that point, but since this one came with serious real estate, there was surely room for one more, whatever the species.

The cage was big, clunky, and homemade, about six feet across and five feet tall. I stood on the sidewalk considering: if I were to attach it to the converted shed I used as an aviary for zebra finches, it would be like adding a covered porch where the birds could get sunlight and feel the breeze.

A warm and friendly woman answered the door. She seemed delighted that I was willing to haul away the cumbersome cage. She went off to fetch the "free bird" incentive.

He was an absolutely gorgeous finch with a shiny ebony head, a forest-green back, and a vibrant purple chest—a Lady Gouldian finch, she told me. They are stunning little five-inch birds native to Australia, with vivid jewel-toned colorings from green to purple to gold. Since the Academy Awards ceremony was airing in a few hours, I decided to name him Oscar. Maneuvering the cage home with a truck and two helpers was so difficult and time consuming that I had to return the following morning to pick up the bird.

I knocked at the door. This time, the friendly woman did not even show her face. Instead, a pair of hands reached out the door, holding a cardboard box, which was taped tightly shut and had a few air holes poked in the lid. The suddenly reclusive donor shut the door abruptly as I was thanking her. As soon as I got home, I opened the box. Oscar? Even to my untrained eye, I could tell this wasn't the same bird I'd been shown the night before. This finch looked as if he'd gone through a few dozen rinse and spin cycles. All the color had been wrung out of his feathers. His head was gray, his back was faded green, and his breast looked like a white tuxedo shirt that had yellowed with age. But his eyes were bright and he looked directly at me, unafraid. Clearly, the nice lady had pulled the old bait and switch.

I had planned to put the original Oscar in our finch aviary, but this bedraggled, woebegone specimen needed some close observation. I put him in my office in a wooden hospital cage that I keep for emergencies. He ate well and seemed healthy, but he was quiet and inactive. Most finches are lively and ceaseless explorers. Oscar was more interested in watching me as I moved around the office. After three weeks of observation, I concluded that he was probably healthy and that his inactivity could be due to loneliness. Finches are flock birds. They need like-feathered company.

One sunny morning, I released Oscar into the aviary inhabited by a dozen zebra finches, gregarious little red-beaked birds with distinctive black-and-white striping. As I had hoped, Oscar became animated once he was in their company. He hopped around the aviary floor, exploring every inch. The zebra finches landed one by one, looked him over, and accepted him on the spot. I checked on Oscar several times during the day. Now that he had company, he became a gregarious, energetic flock member. That changed at nighttime: When the zebra finches flew up to the highest perches to roost, Oscar didn't join them. He spent that evening and the next on the floor, huddled on top of the seed dish in the corner.

Was he being bullied? At dusk, I lurked out of sight near the aviary to try to identify the culprit. All thirteen finches ate their dinner with gusto and preened their side and back feathers. Then one by one they flew to the high perches until only Oscar was left on the ground. He flapped his wings over and over and over again. He could achieve liftoff but was able to rise only an inch or two off the ground before falling back down. He tried and tried until exhaustion forced him to stop. Oscar hopped slowly to the corner seed dish, tucked his head under his wings, and fell asleep.

I admired his moxie, but a flightless bird can be vulnerable—fatally so. Handicapped birds usually don't survive very long, even in a protected aviary. Either they are harassed by other birds or they succumb to disease because they are usually confined to the floor, which is the dirtiest part of an aviary. I considered transferring him back to an inside cage, but he clearly needed company. I'd just have to get him off the ground.

I decided to improvise a low corner perch made from a bamboo gardening stake. When I walked into the aviary to work on it, the zebras panicked and flew up to the highest roosts. Oscar calmly stood his ground and watched. I threaded the bamboo stake through the wire holes on one side of the cage corner and prepared to cut it to the proper size. Oscar hopped up on the perch before I had fastened the other end. Now what?

Oscar showed no fear as we sat next to each other. He stayed firmly seated on the makeshift perch, so I decided to leave it in place. I put another piece of bamboo through the wires in order to get another measurement, but before I pulled it out, Oscar had hopped upward to this second perch. By then he was about five inches off the ground. Instead of looking at me, his gaze had swiveled two inches up, to a point in the wire where he could reach another perch—if some slow-witted human placed it there right away.

I realized what Oscar had in mind. I had brought several

stakes of different diameters and lengths with me, and I ended up using them all. Quickly we developed a routine: Oscar would gaze fixedly at the optimal spot, and I'd put another stake there, a couple of inches up from the last. We continued building a ladder together, with a few delays owing to human error. Sometimes I placed a perch a bit too high for him to reach. Oscar would try, but when he failed to make the distance, he would settle on the perch below and stare at the right spot until I corrected my mistake.

I ran out of stakes a couple of feet from the aviary's highest perches. Oscar spent one more night on the ground, and the following morning I came back with more wooden dowels. We repeated our routine: Oscar would direct me with his stare, I would add the next rung, and he would test-hop to it. It took twenty-eight perches to build Oscar's ladder, but when it was finished, he was able to access some of the highest roosting places in the aviary. Every trip up and down took stamina and patience, but Oscar was game.

Over the months, the drab little castaway flourished. By the end of the next molting season, Oscar had grown a glossy new set of feathers. I had hoped that better feathering would enable him to fly, but it did not. He continued to use his ladder to get to perches when he wanted to take a nap or retire for the night. The zebra finches treated Oscar as a full member of their flock. They were equally accepting of Gail, a middle-aged female Lady Gouldian finch whom I adopted from a local humane society.

Gail had languished there because her head was bald and she was not desired as a pet. One handsome, flightless suitor didn't think this detracted from her appeal.

I didn't provide nest boxes for the finches, since I normally don't let rescued birds breed; there are too many unknowns, such as the reason for Oscar's disability. But Oscar and Gail outsmarted me. They managed to put together a straw nest inside a decorative ceramic gourd that I'd hung from the aviary ceiling. Their love shack was right next to the highest rung on Oscar's ladder. Oscar and Gail produced five radiant babies. All could fly and all had fully feathered heads.

In the end, Oscar proved to be the resourceful architect of his own destiny. The pair's strong drive to reproduce was also propitious. In a backyard aviary that would eventually turn its focus toward the conservation of endangered bird species, these two were way ahead of the game.

Lady Gouldian finches were first discovered in Australia in the mid-nineteenth century by the ornithological artist John Gould, who named them after his wife, Elizabeth. Living in flocks, the birds are nomadic dwellers that move through tropical savannas, depending on the availability of food and water. By 1992, a species population once estimated in the millions had dwindled to a mere twenty-five hundred; such a steep decline qualified Lady Gouldians as endangered in the wild. In Australia, many thousands are being raised in captivity, but despite conservation efforts, their wild population continues to decrease as they are beset by new diseases and large, destructive fires in their native forests.

Though he was the first of his species to land here, Oscar now lives in a large flock of Lady Gouldians on our property; some of them are his offspring. He remains a genial, hail-fellow-well-met kind of guy. When breakfast is served, Oscar is one of the first birds at the communal dish. He especially likes hard-boiled eggs. Instead of quietly nibbling from the edges of the bowl, like some of the shier birds, Oscar jumps straight into the middle of it. Within seconds he is usually joined by so many others that it looks like an avian mosh pit. At night he sleeps huddled between two of his flock mates on a perch that is almost seven feet off the ground. Sleeping position is a status symbol within some species. The more powerful birds get the higher, safer spots; others range up (or down) in order of importance. Oscar's spot is a couple of rungs below the highest perching branch—not bad for a flock member who can't even fly.

I'm sure that Oscar's former owner had no clue what a tiny dynamo she pawned off in that sealed box. Oscar is a planner, a good citizen, and most of all a gifted trans-species communicator. He told me exactly what he needed to stay alive and well. His calm, determined gumption has also been an inspiration for me as I have navigated the closed, nearly all-male society of exotic-bird breeders who made it clear when I started out that there was little room on their lofty perch for a novice female aviculturist.

There were also few manuals on caring for these birds. I realized early on that I would largely have to teach myself the knowledge to care for and breed exotic species; it would come slowly, with a lot of improvisation. When I enrolled in a course on egg incubation at SeaWorld, San Diego I met an instructor and Curator of Birds at the Los Angeles Zoo named Susie Kasielke, who helps restore endangered California condors to the wild. As we discussed their captive breeding program for those giant birds, she told me frankly, "We're trying to reproduce the results; we can't reproduce the process."

That gave me some comfort. I can't give my birds the conditions they have in the wild, but I can help them have a future for their species and provide a good, fulfilled, enriched, and natural life. I do much of that by experimenting, and I embrace the serendipity that brings hurt, endangered, and abandoned creatures my way. At bottom, I've adopted the "can do" tao of Oscar: whatever works.

More than anything, Oscar still helps me appreciate the wit, resilience, and wisdom of birds. His bright, fixed stare is a constructive reminder: Pay attention. Look hard; listen better. We'll all be better off. Now, the Lady Gouldian aviary is so active and full that it's sometimes hard to find Oscar in the frantic morning scrum around the food bowl. That's as it should be, and I am so glad. The giveaway cage that first lured me proved to be too damaged and clunky to use. It was worthless and we junked it. But Oscar, the flightless, one-ounce treasure, is a keeper.

# ONE

# Morning at Pandemonium

I rise every morning just after 4:00 a.m.—gladly on most days—and pad as silently as possible across the terra-cotta-tiled floors of our home. If I make the smallest sound as I pass by the dining room, they might hear. I don't want to set off our resident clown posse—not yet.

"Hello? Want out! I love you!"

Darn. Shana is awake. I ignore her squawky blandishments, and she tries harder.

"Pretty mama, pretty mama. I love you!"

I smile to myself and wait her out. Finally, silence returns. As I finish a mug of tea and an hour of administrative work in my office, dawn flares over the foothills of the Santa Cruz range to our west. Every morning at first light, I step outside into the bewitching bird music that heralds another day at Pandemonium Aviaries, the home and bird sanctuary that I share with my family, two donkeys, a pair of goats, a collie, a sheepdog, one understandably aloof elder cat, and some of the world's most remarkable birds.

Ours is a global birdsong. As I stand on the deck, the morning music begins with a few tentative peeps and soft trills until a full symphony swells from the most vocal of over three hundred avian throats representing over forty species. It knocks me out, every day.

"Whooo, whooo." The Guinea turacos greet the first rays of sun and preen their bright green plumage. They look like Vegas showgirls, with exaggerated white eyeliner and extravagant plumes atop their heads. "Whooo."

Beneath their fluting I can hear the contrapuntal coos of our male ringneck doves as they begin another day of relentless courting, bowing to their lady loves between notes. We also have bleeding-heart doves, Australian crested doves, emerald doves, Senegal doves, and crested quail-doves.

Now Olivia and Ferguson, a pair of majestic East African crowned cranes, are stretching white-tipped wings that span six feet. Electrifying crowns of gold filaments flare from black tufts atop their heads; their eyes, set in a black mask above crimson cheeks, are a piercing cobalt hue. The cranes' low, loud call travels far through the misty hills here. It's the primal sound of morning in the Lake Victoria basin of East Africa, ever fainter there as those habitats grow more perilous for the cranes.

The big birds' trumpeting has roused the rainbow lorikeets, an antic Australian parrot family of mom, dad, and three babies splashed with gaudy primary colors. They pop up groggily from their nesting box, then snap into their frenetic punk-rock personae, screeching, "Harli! Harli! Harli!" as they pogo up and down on their perches.

They're all housed in a sprawling complex of cupolas, turrets, and tropical-hued mosaic-trimmed cages. Pandemonium is a nonprofit focused on saving bird species from extinction through conservation and education. We began as a place where rescued birds could live out their lives without ever having to be moved again. As a rescue organization we could save individual birds, but when we made the transition to conservation breeding, our mission became saving species. In a short time, with primarily volunteer staffing, we have assembled some of the largest flocks of certain rare and exotic species in the world, right in our backyard.

Some of our birds are in far more peril than others. During the morning serenade, I always listen closely for an eerie sonic boom that sends a deep tympanic roll beneath the reedy melodies. Until I hear it, I wonder: Are they awake? Are they okay?

"*Boooooooom.*" There they are. "*Boom, boom, boooom.*"

Early on, I developed a hopeless infatuation with our vivid blue Victoria crowned pigeons, and I fret about them constantly. They are native to New Guinea and they are the largest pigeon species in the world. At a foot and a half, they are just a bit smaller than their extinct forebears from Mauritius, the dodoes. The Victoria crowneds' lacy head plumage looks like a headdress of delicate blue snowflakes fanned above vivid red eyes. At times, they bob their blue-gray fan-shaped tails rhythmically as they vocalize the species' quieter call. It's much like a hum. Some visitors have likened it to a cell phone set on vibrate. For me, the sound whispers of the ancestral, fog-bathed tropical forests of New Guinea. Ours is the second-largest flock of Victoria crowned under conservation in the world. We have grown it bird by bird with our own hatchlings and acquisitions from breeders and zoos. All our birds were bred half a world away from the habitats where their wild ancestors were first trapped or netted and sent off in shipping crates to the United States. Many millions of wild birds have died during capture or in transit—collateral damage in the exotic-creature trade.

We never accept illegally wild-caught birds, but we work hard to ensure the survival of birds who are already in the United States and their offspring. Someday, if we can raise healthy new flocks, these birds may be repatriated to those far-away forests—what's left of them. For now, we aim to keep the species alive, well, and safely reproducing.

The Victoria crowned pigeons, their close relatives blue crowned pigeons, Nicobar pigeons, and the green-naped pheasant pigeons, also from New Guinea, are Pandemonium's main breeding focus. New Guinea is home to the third-largest rain forest in the world. An alarming amount of forest on the huge island has been destroyed, much of it slashed and cleared for palm plantations. Growers are rushing to produce more red palm oil, praised as a carotene-rich "diet miracle" by manufacturers and Web and TV health gurus. There are already plantations producing red palm oil sustainably in countries such as Thailand, Malaysia, and Liberia, as well as in parts of New Guinea. Conservationists have campaigned to identify these responsible vendors on packaging labels, but the habitat encroachment continues at an alarming rate.

What price, this quest for human wellness? The World Wildlife Fund report released in 2011 identified red palm oil cultivation as one of the major threats to wildlife in New Guinea. Like the iguanas, albatross, and giant tortoises so cherished on the Galápagos, two-thirds of the wildlife in New Guinea is believed to be unique in all the world. But unlike the Galápagos Islands, which are rich in ecotourists, poverty-stricken New Guinea has few resources for conservation. So it's possible that the last wild flocks of our New Guinea species will soon go the way of the dodo.

Taking care of some of these rare birds involves a scary amount of guesswork. How does one hand-feed a newly hatched green-naped pheasant pigeon? What's the proper humidity in which to incubate a Victoria crowned pigeon egg? There's plenty to puzzle about in our noisy backyard. Not the least of it is just how all this happened. Mucking out parrot poop is not a predictable second career for me, a former Silicon Valley executive with a master's in management science. Nor is our otherwise "normal" suburban house a likely spot for a sanctuary. Where our kids once gleefully dove into dirt piles, we have built our ever-expanding complex of aviaries—thirty-four large ones and still counting. The garage is now crammed with incubators, caged birds on "hospital watch," and a few thousand live, homegrown mealworms. Never did I think I'd get excited when FedEx delivered an avian fecal test kit.

Some days, the learning curve seems to bend straight up. I'm not sure we could persist were it not for the moments of absolute joy: The fluttering ecstasy of two love-starved turacos finally united as a mated pair. The comic nannyhood of a "bachelor" red-rumped parrot from Australia who insists on helping to raise the chicks of our rosella pairs. We call him Uncle Dutch. His dogged indulgence toward other species' chicks and fully fledged offspring has mystified visiting ornithologists. Dutch is our own species- and gender-confused Mrs. Doubtfire. I love to watch him sneak treats to the older fledglings when their parents aren't looking. Then there is Abraham, a small rock pebbler parrot with a mission. Whenever new birds seem agitated at their unfamiliar surroundings, Abraham welcomes them with a calming mantra: "It's okay, it's okay, it's okaaaaay."

Often, I close my eyes as the morning music rises to full pitch. Some days, the kaleidoscopic beauty of our birds is almost too much as they flit and swoop through the fresh-cut manzanita branches and live shrubbery in their aviaries. They are plumed, tufted, and rakishly "mohawked," striped, spotted, scarlet, turquoise, lime green, orange. Visitors ooh and aah; schoolchildren squeal when the African cranes peer down at them from their favorite high perches. Some of our neighbors drop by to have a look at new arrivals and just stare, transfixed.

It's easy to get lost in the extravagant op art whorled through a single pheasant tail feather.

Our birds are gorgeous. But that's not why I've fallen for them so hard and so deeply. I've learned that their behavior is far more fascinating than their plumage. What birds know has upended anything I thought I understood about the natural world and our place in it. Birds mourn, they sacrifice, they engage in wicked tricks. They name their babies. They invent, they plot, they cope, and, as you'll see, some of them know devilishly well how to manipulate unsuspecting humans. Beset by the forces of nature and the follies of man, they parry with marvelous wit and resilience. They can teach us volumes about the interrelationships of humans and animals.

After over a decade of this work, I am just learning to speak "bird." I'm no whisperer, no avian Dr. Dolittle. Our birds have taught me how to meet their needs. Since they are such powerful educators, their stories are the heart of this book. Some of their journeys to our backyard can break your heart; their spirit and their revelations amaze and cheer me daily. In sharing their odysseys—and yes, their wisdom—I hope to gently pull the rug from beneath what you think you know about these feathered familiars. I intend to convince you that "birdbrain!" is the finest of compliments.

But first, let's amble through the rest of my morning rounds at Pandemonium—and then to the other side of our rescue operation.

As the dawn chorus subsides and the birds settle into their

day, I walk the serpentine stone-and-gravel paths through our enclosures and aviaries and check them all, a little obsessively perhaps. I didn't have to go to "zoo school" (though I did!) to learn that in aviculture, vigilance is critical, especially during nesting season. There are hidden hazards in the tamest suburban ecosystem. If the African cranes find and gobble slugs, they can get parasites. The bacteria in field mouse droppings can kill a healthy, blue iridescent Nicobar pigeon before you know it is ill.

Once I've looked in on our outside aviary birds, I head back into the house for some comic relief. From the kitchen, I sound reveille to the menagerie of "companion birds"—rescued macaws and other parrots—who spend their nights in floor-to-ceiling aviaries lining our dining room walls.

"Wake up! Time to party!" I call out.

Mayhem erupts in a furious chorus of shrieks, squawks, and wisecracks. They holler back in half a dozen distinct voices.

"Hey, pretty mama!"

"Come on!"

"Are you hungry?"

"Hello. Hello. Hello."

"Hello" (in an English accent).

"Uh-oh!"

"Do you want a cappuccino?"

"Want out!"

Should my husband, Tom, pass through on his way to work,

Amigo, a red-headed Amazon parrot, is liable to cock his head and train a gimlet eye. I cringe, knowing what's coming. Amigo is a grumpy old guy in his forties or older. He's been with us the longest and somehow he has it in for my very patient and supportive spouse. Tom always gets a sweet and personal greeting:

"Asshole!"

Some of the dining room crew can cuss a deep blue streak; others call plaintively for their lost owners: "Come get me. Mimi? Roger!" With life spans that can stretch from forty to seventy years depending on the species, many companion birds simply outlive their owners. On average, a long-lived parrot will cope with nine new homes and many difficult readjustments. All our noisy adoptees have had their primary relationships sundered by the tides of human frailty and misfortune: old age, home foreclosure, job loss, AIDS, cancer, heart disease, poverty, or flat-out cruelty. A good number have arrived sick or injured. Most of our rescued companion birds come from shelters and rescue groups, but some have been private adoptions.

All the parrots and macaws have deep backstories, some as dark and unknowable as the secrets of our wild birds. We don't dwell on that here. It's all about healing—and joy. That's why we begin our days with a song-and-dance fest.

"Hey, guys!" I chirp, boom box in hand. "Merry Christmas!"

I play what I've seen them respond to. Lately, every morning is Christmas, regardless of the season. The holiday songs they like best are fast and catchy, drawn mostly from fifties pop. "I Saw

Mommy Kissing Santa Claus" is a perennial favorite. Another chestnut: Brenda Lee's "Rockin' Around the Christmas Tree":

> Everyone's dancing merrily
> In the new old-fashioned way.

I can't tell you why the birds fell into a permanent Christmas groove, just that it persists. It began in early December about two years ago. The weather had been chilly and rainy for weeks, and we were all cranky. I turned on the radio, and the first channel I hit was blasting "Jingle Bells." Even parrots that normally don't sing and dance started bobbing their heads in perfect time to the music.

I knew we were onto something. The birds take their dancing and singing very seriously, and music selection is key. If they think a song stinks, they'll perch, unmoving, and glare or peck sulkily at their food bowls. When they heard that first Christmas carol, none of them even paused for a snack or a sip of water.

These birds can boogie. Not all of them dance, but no one here has trained those that do. Our dancers are naturals, grooving smack on the beat. Some macaws pop and lock on their perches like hip-hop MCs. If they're dancing outside their cages, the African gray parrots form a conga line on the floor. It's our private indulgence. We have no YouTube cameras livestreaming our dancefests, no audience at all except for Amadeus and Kenya, our Lady Ross's turaco and violaceous turaco, whose aviary is just outside the dining room window. They peek in from their perches and sometimes bob along. Amadeus came to us with just one leg. That curbs any dancing but doesn't seem to affect his joie de vivre.

When "Jingle Bells" finished on that first day of what would become endless Christmases, the rest of the gang waited patiently for the next cut. Only Mylie, a ravishing but emotionally immature Catalina macaw, was unmoved by the Christmas tunes. She sat back and watched the others perform, haughty as a queen amused by her jesters. As the Ronettes' version of "Frosty the Snowman" started, the flock exploded with enthusiasm. Finally, I was giving them material they could work with, music that had the right beat and a perfect mixture of simple and complicated vocals. All singers could keep pace but remain challenged. Now I can't imagine we'll ever take Christmas out of our repertoire. We enjoy it too much.

I don't care what I must look like, bopping along with a bird on each arm. I've led our daily dance party for several years now. Before we settled into holiday music, we'd shaken our tail feathers to all genres. We still mix the playlists for variety—and my sanity. They include rock and roll, the Beatles, salsa, reggae, and enough Disney tunes to drive any adult human around the bend and back. A favorite is *Disney's Princess Collection.* Cinderella! Ariel! Jasmine! Snow White! Belle! Bring on the schmaltz.

When it all gets too much, I cut the treacle and cue up James Brown's funky anthem "I Feel Good."

Tico, a handsome male blue and gold macaw, is our best dancer, bold and tempestuous as a flamenco artist. When he's in the mood, he can move his head and body in opposite directions, riffing on a belly dance he developed for one of the Disney numbers. A more recent resident, Shana, a twenty-nine-year-old yellow-naped Amazon female, was at first stubbornly resistant to the music and mayhem. Her arrival provided a sad and unsettling crash course on helping parrots traumatized by losing their homes.

We had some harrowing nights with Shana. At first, her cage was in the spare bedroom near ours. At about 4:00 a.m., I was awakened by Shana singing the iconic opening of Beethoven's Fifth Symphony. "Duh-duh-duh DAAAAH!" She trilled through the first few measures, note-perfect. Her voice has the operatic power required for this commanding piece.

The Central American, Costa Rican, and southern Mexican rain forests to which her species is native were noisy places supporting large flocks of flashy psittacines, but those areas have become much quieter as yellow-naped parrots encounter habitat destruction and illegal capture for the pet trades. Yellow-napeds are prized as pets both for their intelligence and for their impressive talking and singing abilities. They have a great sense of pitch—though Shana can let loose a clunker every now and then.

Despite my approach in that wee hour on tiptoes, Shana

stopped singing. Her hearing, like that of most parrots, is quite acute. "Good morning!" she called out with gusto.

Shana took my silence as a sign that the approaching human needed some enticement.

"Are you hungry?" she asked. Then she lapsed into a cartoony voice, repeating a silly chorus: "Oh, it's a birdie!"

When I peeked into the room and flicked on a dim light, Shana shrieked at the sight of me. "Mimi! Robert!" she yelled in her panic. "Mimi! Robert! Come here!"

Mimi and Robert were Shana's loving family for all but the first year of her life. A childless, active couple, they spent their free time outdoors either gardening or biking or hiking, nearly always with Shana in tow. Shana had been their darling; their photo albums show Shana on the handlebars of a bicycle, at the beach, at a birthday party. But the couple wanted a lifestyle change and Shana didn't fit into the shimmering new picture, so they brought her to me.

Unless we could help her, she faced decades of lonely maladjustment. Abandonment is always difficult. Even birds that have been in bad homes can have a hard time adjusting to a new family. They mourn, they get angry and have tantrums or bite. Even the most mellow birds don't find the change easy. With such a long connection with one family, Shana was traumatized by the inexplicable and sudden separation from all she knew. She wouldn't let me touch her. If I offered her food treats, she threw them on the floor.

For lack of a better tactic, I tried to gentle her back toward comfort and trust. In the softest voice that was still audible, I repeated a soothing phrase: "You're all right, Shana. You're all right." It seemed to help a little. After a while, she stopped screaming for Mimi and Robert and began to comfort herself with a mantra. "Pretty bird. Pretty bird," she chanted softly. I began to keep a diary of her daily actions, hoping to discover any small signs of progress. Flipping the pages was of little comfort. After weeks of angrily flinging away any treat, Shana finally consented to hold an offering for a few seconds before letting it drop to the floor of her cage. When I reached my hand out and asked her to step up, she hesitated before turning her back to me.

Then, finally, a real breakthrough. Shana began joining the parrot dancefest in the mornings, just singing to the music. If I looked directly at her, she'd stop singing right away. The page in my diary entry recording her first group participation is covered with exclamation points. But it was a momentary triumph. For the next three mornings, she stayed mute when I put on the music. If I approached her cage, she started calling for Mimi and Robert again and calming herself with "pretty bird."

I don't normally use that sort of parrot cliché with my birds, but I had nothing else to throw at this problem. I'd heard Mimi say "pretty bird" to Shana just before she walked out of her life. I practiced until I was as close to Mimi in tone and intonation as I could remember, and I kept it up: "You're such a pretty bird, Shana." She seemed calmed by the phrase and the sing-song cadence, repeating after me, "Pretty bird," like a child soothing itself by stroking a well-loved stuffed animal.

We were at this standstill for several weeks; it wasn't a happy time. I was angry at the couple for Shana's pain and at myself for being unable to help her more. Stewing was hardly productive, but I'd simply run out of ideas. One morning, over six months after Shana's arrival, I approached her cage as usual, opened the door, and held out my forearm for one more try, saying, "Hi, pretty bird. You're such a pretty bird, Shana. Want to go outside?"

She stepped up onto my forearm as if it were the most natural thing in the world and greeted me: "Hello, pretty mama."

Well, rock my world, little girl. I still love my "new" name, which has stuck with Shana from that moment. Mostly I'm grateful that she has begun trusting another human. It was clearly her decision, in her own good time. To my greater joy, her grief has receded enough for a new relationship—with me. She is indeed a pretty bird: pretty special, pretty brave, and pretty wonderful—even if she can't dance worth a darn. She did try, and she seemed to know it was hopeless. She finally gave up and just started belting out, "Dashing through the snow," at operatic volume—if slightly off-key.

As Shana wails away, I love to waltz with Beakman, a female

blue and gold macaw who arrived with her own set of physical and emotional problems. She came to Pandemonium after having been kept indoors and all but motionless in a small cage for seventeen years. Her toenails were badly overgrown, which greatly reduced her range of motion. She was fed mainly peanuts and did not like to be touched—at all.

Despite this misguided husbandry, Beakman's owner, Archie, maintained that he did love her, very much. He was in tears when he called to explain that he was losing his home, and he was frantic about her fate. He had placed an ad on Craigslist to find her a new place to live, and the first caller made it clear that he wanted the bird for "mixed species fighting." Archie was appalled and quickly withdrew the ad. When he was finally evicted, I brought Beakman home. Even after her nails were trimmed, balance was a big problem for her in the beginning. Now she has recovered to such an extent that she'll dance every chance she gets.

The morning dance party always ends with a procession to the birds' outdoor aviaries. Sometimes I move them all myself, singly or in pairs. Sometimes an intern arrives early and they'll go out on his or her capable arms. I need to return to the huge task of getting meals ready and delivered. Feeding all those birds takes four hours daily. My kitchen is filled with cases of papaya, blueberries, melon, grapes. We buy or are given seed by the pallet.

At about 9:00 a.m., all our interns start to troop in. They

come from colleges, veterinary programs, and the local community. They help with website development, volunteer coordination, fund-raising events, and research. Some interact directly with the birds. Depending on their experience level, they clean cages, assist with feeding and medicating, and conduct experimental sessions in "parrot enrichment," teaching the companion birds more language and shape recognition.

As the interns head off to their tasks, I put together the first heavy tray of food bowls. From the corral out back, a donkey brays, and a blue-feathered wise guy snaps back, "Shut up!"

Tico, my bad boy. Tico the trickster, the skilled and sneaky lock picker, the practical joker, the heartbreaker. Tico the merciless mimic. Now he's mocking poor Trixie, one of the donkeys: "*Heeeeehawwwawww.* Heh-heh-heh."

"Pandemonium" fits our operation, no doubt about it. Tom and I let the children choose the organization's name from a list of possibilities. We figured that we owed them the privilege. They've endured parrots grooming their hair and shrieking through their favorite TV shows. They've bounced in from school ravenous and bitten into what looked like corn bread but was in fact yucky home-baked "birdie bread." Too many mornings, they've seen Mom sleepless and cranky during the tense and busy nesting season. When I gave them the list of possible names, I made my favorite known: Paz y Amor, Spanish for Peace and Love.

*Really,* Mom? If there's been any sibling rivalry in our home over the years, it's been between the kids and those Mom-hogging birds. With little debate, their vote was for the obvious choice. We learned only later that *pandemonium* is also the accepted collective noun or "flock name" (as in *gaggle of geese, covey of doves*) for a group of parrots.

Having found *pandemonium* such a felicitous choice, we looked up other flock names. Just a sampling of what we found:

> *a wisdom of owls*
> *a murder of crows*
> *an ascension of larks*
> *an unkindness of ravens*
> *a siege of herons*
> *an ostentation of peacocks*
> *a mob of emus*
> *a parliament of rooks*
> *a lamentation of swans*

As these collective nouns show, we humans certainly have diverse impressions of these creatures of the sky. We credit some with beauty and wisdom and blithely defame others. Our attitudes toward them are complicated and our understanding so fragmented. How much better our relationships could be if it weren't quite so one sided. I listen closely to our birds, and I talk to them all the time, even if it's to whisper to the tiniest and frailest of them, "Come on. Live!"

Sometimes, when I've been up all night with a struggling

hatchling, I do wonder at the burden of hope we place on our small ark of survivors. You can't do this sort of work without a lot of internal debate—especially in those lonely small hours. It's hard to find words for the compulsion to know and protect this improbable flock. A hundred and fifty years ago, when Emily Dickinson wrote the poem so many generations of schoolchildren have learned by rote, she couldn't have dreamed it would have fresh meaning as an avian conservationist's prayer. It works for me and for our mission at Pandemonium.

> "Hope" is the thing with feathers—
> That perches in the soul—
> And sings the tune without the words—
> And never stops—at all—

# TWO

# One Dove Leads
# to Another, and Another . . .

I had never held a bird before. Yet there I was by the side of the Lawrence Expressway near Santa Clara, dressed in crisp new gym togs and cradling a trembling white dove. It seemed badly hurt. As it lay against my palm, I could feel its panicked heartbeat; my own was racing as well. Balanced there amid the noise and hot wind of traffic and the blinding afternoon light, I felt a bit disoriented. The tall, well-chiseled man who stood beside me looked anxiously at his watch.

I had set out just after lunch that day with a modest suburban mom's resolve: Time to get back into shape. Our boys were growing, but I was determined that my hips and thighs would not. Though I was and still am an enthusiastic hiker, I had come up with a less conventional discipline to get myself fit again. I decided that I would lift weights—and not those dainty sets of dumbbells at a measly twelve pounds each. I meant the really heavy bar that you heave up over your head. I wanted to learn Olympic-style lifting, the kind with chalk on your hands, metal clanging, big weights thudding to the mat. Grunts. Moans. Bring it on!

I had joined a gym that offered a promotion for three free training sessions. Matt, the trainer assigned to me, was six feet five, with zero body fat and a totally professional manner. Yet Matt was a no-show for our second appointment—or he was just very, very late. I paced, and then I fumed. I was about to take myself off in a Gore-Tex huff when he ran up from the parking lot and apologized. There was this bird . . .

On his way to the gym, he explained, he had noticed a white dove by the side of the highway. It was flapping its wings piteously but unable to right itself or fly. Traffic roared past a few feet away. Matt was torn: there was a time-pressed, auburn-haired woman waiting with a "free session" voucher who must be served if he was to keep his job, and there was the wounded bird. He sped past the pathetic sight, thought better of it, took the next exit and doubled back. Gently, he moved the dove out of harm's way and laid her beneath a bush. And there he was, apologizing to me for his late arrival. Since Matt was probably expecting a tart rebuke, my question must have been a relief.

"Would you mind if we checked on the bird?" He didn't hesitate. "I'll drive," he answered, and we headed toward the place where he'd left the dove. Minutes later, there I was, on the side of the highway, lifting that few ounces of feathers and fear. She craned her neck to look up at me. I was a goner, though I didn't realize it at the time.

Most of us can point to fateful moments in our lives—turning points, enlightenments, the misty dawn of true love. But few of us recognize them without the wisdom of hindsight. As they're happening, these moments can seem mundane, or completely absurd. So it was with the first glimmers of Pandemonium on that sunny afternoon in 1996. I just looked like a crazy lady by the side of a highway.

It took us nearly an hour to locate a clinic with an avian vet, the only bird specialist within thirty miles. In that pre–smart phone era, Matt had stopped and checked a directory. When he called, they told him to come straight in. During the drive to the clinic, the dove fell asleep in my lap. Had I ever looked at a bird so closely? This one was pure white except for a faint beige-pink tinge around its eyes and beak. The feathers were surprisingly varied up close. Some were long and tapered for navigation; the head and neck plumage was short and silky smooth. The wings were furled against her body in perfect geometry, smooth and snowy white. She was lovely, very still, and barely breathing. I saw no obvious injuries.

I knew almost nothing about any birds, not even the names of the ones singing in my garden. They were free, self-sufficient creatures with lives and concerns that soared way above my head. Certainly I hadn't imagined this trembling vulnerability, or its power to move me. I know now that if the dove had struggled when I picked it up, I might have killed it by tightening my grip. In order for birds to breathe, muscles in the chest must be able to push the sternum outward. Impeding that movement by holding a bird too firmly around the rib cage can fatally stop its airflow.

At the clinic, we were quickly waved through a waiting area with yapping Yorkies and lunging spaniels. I could feel the dove's heartbeat quicken again as I held it safely above the commotion. We were ushered into an examining room and into the care of Dr. Sara Varner, a middle-aged woman with dark, curly hair pulled back into a practical ponytail. As she took the bird from me, I felt an almost physical relief. The dove was someone else's problem now, poor thing. Matt was out in the lobby, phoning his next client and my babysitter. I hoped the treatment wouldn't take too long.

"No, it's not my bird," I told the vet. "It must have been hit by a car." The exam began with the basics I recognized from the countless visits I'd made with our many family dogs and cats. The dove was weighed, its heartbeat checked, its body gone over nimbly by the doctor's practiced hands. She lifted a wing, then said, "I thought so. Look at this." She held the wing up carefully so that I could peer at the area to which she pointed. Two small punctures beneath the bird's wing were rimmed with dried blood. "This bird wasn't hit by a car. It was dropped by a hawk."

What colossal bad luck, to be pierced with talons midair, then dropped from a great height. How ruthless an undoing— but somehow not quite as random and unjust as being smashed by a speeding Toyota, I figured. What was that phrase? "Nature, red in tooth and claw." Dr. Varner pointed out that it was nesting season for wild birds and that it was likely the hawk was on its way to feed fledglings when something made it abandon its prey. The babies might have gone hungry as a result. I was adjusting my perspective on the sad affair when Dr. Varner continued, with some heat in her voice: "These domesticated white doves don't stand a chance in the wild. Their color makes them stand out, and the hawks have an easy time targeting them."

The bird could have escaped from a backyard dovecote. Or it could have been thrust into the wild after its part in a romantic wedding ceremony, a sacrifice that the bird might have been bred and sold for. Dove release has become a popular coda to outdoor "I do's." It's a pretty sight, but I had never considered the aftermath. Though doves are sent aloft to herald a couple's upbeat future, the birds can be headed for an ugly fate. Unskilled in finding food, they might starve or end up as an aerial predator's meal. Some die in traffic or by contact with electrical lines.

The vet's prognosis was grim. Deep, multiple puncture wounds caused by the hawk's talons gave this bird little chance for survival. Dr. Varner respectfully suggested euthanasia. When a hurt wild bird such as a pigeon is brought to her clinic, she directs the person who brought it in to the nearest wildlife rescue organization. Most likely the bird will be euthanized there, but a small number do get saved.

Pet birds found escaped and injured—say, a parrot hit by a car—will be sent to the local humane society with ties to a bird rescue group. Rescue organizations seldom turn down any bird in need; they'll probably bring it back to Dr. Varner for treatment at a discounted fee. Once the bird has healed, the rescue group will try to arrange an adoption.

The dove—neither pet nor wild, so badly hurt, and unclaimed—faced the poorest odds. A shelter wouldn't even try to treat it, and there was almost no chance of survival. So why not end it now? Transferring a badly injured domesticated dove to a shelter where it was certain to be killed would merely prolong its pain and suffering. Dr. Varner would have done what many vets routinely do with a badly injured wild bird. She would have wrung its neck. Such an end was quick, merciful, and mindful of the tough economics of animal rescue.

I absorbed all the logic. I'm sure I did.

"Please, please try to save her," I pleaded. "I'll pay even though she's not my bird." The vet hesitated. Finally, reluctantly, she said, "Leave the bird here. I'll do what I can."

From her makeshift gurney—a towel set in a plastic container—the dove looked directly at me. She lay still, almost serene, as Dr. Varner explained about IVs, heat, and supportive care that involved an oxygen chamber. I hardly took it in, impatient to check back in to my own life. I had nothing at home for dinner and I would have to beg the sitter to stay, pick up my car, dash to the market. Worse, it was almost rush hour. As

Matt and I headed out, Dr. Varner said she would call if there were any changes with my bird.

"*My* bird? No, she's not. But I'd like to know how she is."

I figured that was it.

The next day, after I dropped the kids off at school, I drove the half hour to the clinic to visit the dove. I had no idea why; I simply surrendered to the compulsion. The bird looked up as though she recognized me, struggled to get up, and fell back. But the vet tech had good news: since the dove was able to eat that morning, the antibiotics were probably working against any infection. I kept going back, a full hour of driving for each round-trip. By day three, the dove could stand. Again, she struggled to her feet when she saw me come in. By day four, she was out of the oxygen chamber and breathing well. The next morning, as I finished breakfast with the children, Dr. Varner called.

"I'm very sorry to tell you that your bird died early this morning."

I stammered my thanks for her efforts and hung up. Was I crying? Why? Okay, I'd gotten involved—somewhat. Still, the emotion caught me off guard. I snapped the local newspaper open in front of my face to screen my distress from the kids. Later, I had to admit that my reaction, outsize though it seemed, was pretty much in character. As a child, I had sobbed through *Lady and the Tramp* seven times, inconsolable at the cruel snubbing of Lady's mongrel love interest. Growing up in

Puerto Rico, I was the de facto animal rescue agent in our suburban San Juan neighborhood, the "please can we keep him?" kid who was always bringing home stray cats and dogs.

After I moved to New England for college, then west to the Bay Area in my twenties, I volunteered at animal shelters. I even helped find sanctuary for a baby zoo elephant that was about to be sold to a foreign circus. I've always felt a strong connection with animals, along with a deep revulsion for their suffering at human hands. The truth is, I need them in my life. It's a connection that settles and comforts me in a direct, non-judgmental way that people can't often provide.

As a single businesswoman, I had always had dogs when I could manage it. Once I was married and we found a newly built spec home on one pretty acre in Los Altos, there were rarely fewer than four or five animals underfoot. In the early nineties, after our youngest son, Nick, was born, I had planned to return to my former, quite lucrative career as a venture capital consultant in Silicon Valley. A series of health issues with the children made that untenable. If I was going to stay at home, I was happy to have furry allies to absorb some of the energy and emotion churned up by three boys under seven and Tom's preteen daughter, Lizzy.

It's no surprise that I lacked the fortitude to resist the pair of baby chicks our oldest son, Ross, begged to bring home from a kindergarten "hatching lesson." The fuzzy babies stayed in his room—with Ross taking them for daily outdoor play sessions—until they were feathered. By then it was clear that we had a rooster and a hen, and a potential dynasty in the making. Ross didn't take it well when we told him his birds would have to move outdoors. So when we had a coop built, I promised him it would look just like a comfy extension of the house. Inside we hung a funky iron chandelier with welded farm animal shapes that I had found at a garage sale, and there was a porch with an old wicker sofa.

That airy, decorated chicken coop was a prototype of sorts for the sixty-three fanciful, themed aviaries that have since gone up around it. To me, creature comfort is a basic right. All beings in my care should have clean, safe, attractive surroundings; all should be allowed to "walk in beauty," as the Navajo say. Captivity, even for safety and conservation purposes, is a thorny issue. So why not soften wire mesh with eucalyptus branches and live shrubbery? Why not install a soothing fountain, or station a huge Buddha to cast a benevolent gaze over a feed bowl? Why not, every now and then, let the chickens sashay through the kitchen? I suppose that's the insistent question that's tugged at me through scores of subsequent avian adoptions from private owners, breeders, and rescue groups. *Why the heck not?*

There is another, more basic impulse that moves many of us, whether you're an animal shelter volunteer, or you foster a service dog in training, or you raise funds to neuter feral cats—or you're a well-trained avian scientist returning endangered whooping cranes to the wild: somebody needs to do this.

OUR GROWING MENAGERIE had formed a pretty affable community in the backyard. At the end of the day, they would appear in formation outside our glass kitchen door. It was a comic lineup: two dogs at the back, three cats in the middle row, and the chickens up front. The chickens were in charge of pecking at the door to remind me it was dinnertime. Their rat-a-tat was like clockwork.

This controlled chaos made me happy. So why, surrounded by children and animals for the usual raucous breakfast hour, was I still moping about the dove? As I blinked back those surprising tears, I wasn't really reading the paper as much as hiding behind it. I waited to hear the ding of spoons scraping empty cereal bowls. Focus, I told myself, scanning the accounts of flower shows and high school wrestling matches. Boldface lettering caught my eye in an ad: DESPERATELY NEED A HOME FOR A WHITE DOVE. WILL PROVIDE A MONTH'S WORTH OF FOOD.

Kismet. Fate. What were the odds? Maybe I could still "rescue" a dove and even the tally. Once the kids were off to school, I decided to check it out. Though it was just 7:35 a.m., I called the number in the paper, strangely excited. It rang several times before a sleepy woman's voice answered. Her tone brightened when I asked about the dove. She introduced herself as Eileen and said that I should come over straightaway if I wanted to adopt her doves.

Had I heard plural? The ad clearly read "dove." She quickly

reverted to the singular form. Yes, Eileen really loved her dove, but it couldn't coexist with her plan for a new business: wedding-release doves.

I got over there pretty quickly. Eileen's cottage and yard were small, picturesque, and prim; white fences were draped with purple flowering vines. White gravel walkways had tall, white-washed aviaries flanking each side. They were filled with the dazzling flutter of white doves, dozens of them. These were ringneck doves, like the one that had died. Eileen said that she needed their aviary space for a new flock of birds. Everything else was all set; she had fancy filigreed transport cages and an elegant dress to wear when she performed wedding releases. Buying the ringnecks was the only misstep in her business plan.

"I really need white homing pigeons," Eileen explained. "As long as they're white, no one will know the difference."

As I'd soon learn, there really is no appreciable difference between pigeons and doves. They're both names for essentially the same sort of bird, members of the Columbidae family. Within that category, though, there are many species with quite distinct characteristics. Homing pigeons are domesticated rock doves that have been bred over centuries to find their way home across great distances. They can be extraordinary athletes. In 1885, the *New York Times* reported the triumphant return of a cock homing pigeon known as the Red Whizzer, who took 12 days, 23 hours, and 45 minutes to fly 930 miles from Pensacola, Florida, to Philadelphia, a world record at the time. The Whizzer was retired with golden leg bands to commemorate his feat. Flights of double his distance have been recorded since then.

Eileen's requirements called for homing pigeons with a far more modest range for her local business. She realized that she was better off with a boomerang stock, able to find the way home after the weddings, thus saving the cost and disruption of replacement doves. The homing pigeons that she had ordered were due to arrive soon and they needed the real estate.

To be fair, Eileen really was an animal lover—a houseful of pampered Persian cats attested to that. Buying the ringnecks had been an honest mistake. But even homing pigeons released too close to dark at evening weddings can be in serious peril, as navigation can be more difficult. Failing to check for impending storms before a release is another form of negligence. It's enough of a problem that a responsible segment of the industry has developed a bird-handling code of ethics.

"So how many will you take?"

Since I already knew what could happen to wayward doves, Eileen's next tactic was highly effective. "If I don't find a taker for these doves, I'll have to release them. I'll feed them if they come around. But there are hawks in this neighborhood, so I hope I don't have to resort to that."

Was this a cosmic setup or what? I blurted out my sad hawk-and-dove saga. We both sniffled. Eileen's praise for our attempted rescue was capped by a pronouncement worthy of a carnival fortune teller: Didn't I see it? I was meant to have doves.

How about two dozen?

I was resolute: "One dove."

She parried: "Two is the minimum, but it's almost as bad as one. Birds live in societies, just like you and me. How would you feel if for the rest of your life it was just you and one other person?"

I had no comeback for that one, just questions: How would I know how to care for them? How many to a cage? What do they eat? Eileen rattled off information, including why some of her birds were banded. A pair of birds banded with the same color—red, yellow, green, gray, and so on—indicated a mated pair. Females are banded on the left, she explained, and males on the right foot because "males are always right." She did not smile as she said it.

I stood firm at six birds. Eileen began netting them hastily, before I changed my mind. As she began putting the birds into a carton for the trip home, one dove made an odd noise, something like a hiccup.

"Just a little cough," Eileen said. "They're all fine. Doves are easy peasy. " She handed me a slim newsletter from the American Dove Association. "Subscribe to this. It will answer any questions you have."

I WILL NOT dwell on the spirited exchange when Tom came home that evening. My husband is a kind, caring physician, a lung specialist who taught at a university medical school for many years. He has compassion for all living things and an artist's eye for natural beauty; his bold, witty watercolors brighten most rooms in our home. Tom is also a practical man, and even though he longed for a few unorthodox pets of his own—donkeys, goats, and pigs were on his wish list at the time—our lively blended family called for a tight rein on the expenses.

We agreed on some conditions: No more visits to Eileen. And these doves had to cozy into the chicken coop we had built for Ross's adoptees and their offspring. For the first time, but far from the last time, Tom declared, "No new aviaries." If we added some dove perches toward the top and enclosed some adjoining yard, the ten-by-ten-foot shelter seemed big enough for all. It would be a coop-cum-aviary. All was peaceable in that cooing, clucking kingdom until a few days later when I found a green-banded dove dead on the ground, stiff and covered with bloodied peck marks. The band was on its left foot; it was a female. I didn't know whether the chickens had killed her or had pecked her body after she died. I had noticed when I first got the birds home that she was the only green-banded bird in my little flock.

Just days into my watch, a dove was dead. I felt terribly guilty. I wanted to give the doves back to Eileen and called to tell her so. I was crying—again—so it took a while for me to clarify the details of the tragedy.

"You put doves in with chickens?" Eileen bellowed. "What were you thinking? Doves can't defend themselves."

I had to face it: my mistake was as boneheaded but unintentional as Eileen's buying the ringnecks in the first place. When emotions cooled, I had some questions for Eileen. The green-banded bird had behaved differently from the other doves from the start. It stayed separate from the others, never flew, and acted, well, disconsolate. It wouldn't even drink from the watering station like all the other birds. What could that have been about? There was silence on the line for a moment.

"I lost a dove last night," Eileen said quietly. "I found it dead on the floor. It had a green band, too. Right foot."

It was a male; my bird with the green band on the left foot was a female. In her haste to net the birds, she had inadvertently separated them. Ringnecks are monogamous and they mate for life. They can mourn at the death or disappearance of a mate. Some stop eating or drinking. Could these two have perished from grief just a few miles apart? If so, it was a devotion worthy of star-crossed Shakespearean lovers. I wouldn't let myself consider it.

I COULDN'T HAVE known it then, but pigeons and doves would prove as integral to the growth of Pandemonium as these "common" birds have been to the march of human history. I didn't know much at all about the long and complex interrelationships between birds and humans. But I was determined that there would be no more death by ignorance in my house.

For starters, I began reading about the Columbidae family. According to BirdLife International, a global partnership of conservation groups, there are 9,934 existing bird species in the world. Few of them have a closer or richer historical connection to humans than those known as doves and pigeons. They have carried our messages, served as food, and provided fertilizer for thousands of years. They have also had a place in our amusements. Well before people began to race pigeons, they were used in ancient sporting events. The Romans employed pigeons as winged tote boards, sending them aloft from distant finish lines to report the results of chariot races. Greeks sent them into the skies to deliver the results of Olympic Games in the eighth century BC.

I had always heard about hero military dogs and warhorses, but I didn't realize that pigeons were among the earliest animals enlisted in men's infernal wars. That barbarian of legend Genghis Khan larded much of Asia and eastern Europe with messenger pigeon stations to stay abreast of his own conquests.

Over six hundred years later, pigeons came to the aid of Paris, carrying official dispatches across the Prussian lines during the 1870 Siege of Paris. The birds braved extreme cold, gunfire, and Prussian-trained interceptor falcons to carry the lifesaving intelligence. A grateful French nation commissioned Frédéric-Auguste Bartholdi—designer of the Statue of Liberty—to sculpt a bronze monument to the heroic birds. It was erected in the place des Ternes in 1905 to commemorate the birds. (Fittingly, I suppose, the statue was melted down for munitions in World War II).

Hero carrier pigeons have been decorated by grateful armies. In World War I, a pigeon attached to the US Army Signal Corps won France's highest military honor—the Croix de Guerre—in Verdun. Cher Ami, a homing pigeon, saved the Seventy-Seventh Infantry Division's Lost Battalion, which was trapped in a large, trough-like depression, surrounded by German troops, and mistakenly bombarded by friendly fire. Cher Ami delivered a dozen critical messages, including this one from the doomed battalion: "We are along the road parallel 276.4. Our artillery is dropping a barrage directly on us. For heaven's sake stop it."

The desperate American troops watched the bird launch himself with the message and encounter enemy fire. Cher Ami flew twenty-five miles and arrived at his coop bloodied, a bullet to his chest and one leg nearly severed. But attached to the leg was the silver message canister; the shelling stopped, the men were rescued, and 194 lives were saved. Though medics made the bird a wooden leg and the army demobilized him back to the States with a hero's send-off, Cher Ami died of his injuries in 1919. Or perhaps Cher Ami died of *her* injuries. Some sources report that an autopsy revealed that the pigeon was a hen!

Pigeons were conscripted in World War II as well. You've heard of the famous Victory Gardens planted all over America to produce homegrown food? The US Army Signal Corps also put out a call for donated homing pigeons. Professional and backyard fanciers answered the call, and pigeon "troop strength" soared to fifty-two thousand.

Before there were lab rats, pigeons contributed to groundbreaking scientific research. The evolutionary theorist Charles Darwin was fascinated by pigeons. In 1855 he began raising specialty breeds such as pouters, fantails, short-faced tumblers, and carriers at his home in England. In his masterwork, *On the Origin of the Species,* he declared that "the diversity of the breeds is something astonishing."

Darwin's study of pigeon genetics as a means to explore his theory of natural selection has just received an amazing update: Genome scientists are now sequencing DNA in forty pigeon breeds to study just how evolution works. Nearly 150 years later, these new genetic studies support Darwin's contention that all pigeon breeds are descendents of the rock dove, a bird that once ranged from Asia to Europe and North Africa.

Pigeon behavior helped shape modern psychology. B. F. Skinner's work in the field of cognitive behavior proved the power of operant conditioning by experimenting with pigeons. During World War II, Skinner also began training his lab birds to peck at silhouettes of known enemy targets intending to create— yes—the pigeon-guided missile. He whirled his feathered cadets in centrifuges, subjecting them to increased g-forces, loud noises, and flashing lights. Mercifully, for birds and humans, the project was abandoned.

I was surprised to find that military carrier pigeons were still used during the Vietnam War and that pigeons have been trained for helicopter search and rescue missions over the high seas. They have amazing visual acuity. A pigeon's field of vision covers 340 degrees—far greater than that of humans. The bird's small brain also processes what it sees much faster than we can. Pigeons, like horses, are also extremely sensitive to any movement in their field of vision. Given all these visual abilities, pigeons have been shown to be able to spot and react to shipwrecks from high over the seas.

As I've found with the many species we have rescued at Pandemonium, pigeons have been buffeted for centuries by changing human needs and desires. That includes crime. Drug traffickers still send pigeons through the impenetrable gorges between Afghanistan and Pakistan. In India, the fleets of winged message carriers indispensable to remote police stations since 1946 have been given their walking papers, rendered obsolete by the Internet.

Given this history of service, why do they get such a bum rap?

Pigeons' noble assists to humankind make me ashamed—kind of—for having giggled at the Woody Allen line in *Stardust Memories,* which disrespected the ubiquitous city pigeons we're so familiar with as "rats with wings," dirty, messy, disease ridden. What's in a name, if the bird is essentially the same? Doves can be "pure" soaps and premium chocolate brands. In most myth, religion, literature, and visual arts, the Columbidae family members known as doves received far gentler treatment than pigeons. Aphrodite, the Greek goddess of love, was depicted in a chariot pulled by white doves. In Christianity, the Holy Ghost is manifested as a white dove. Early Judaism selected the most pure animals to use as sacrifices, and white doves often won that dubious distinction. In the Old Testament, Noah sent a raven from the ark during the Flood to seek dry land; the raven refused to go. Noah cursed it, then sent a dove. It flew back to the ark bearing an olive branch—land ho!

Understanding my birds' place in human history was fun, and I still like to research all our bird species' behavior, physiology, and interaction with humankind. But with five doves cooing in a new aviary annexed to the chicken coop with Tom's grudging consent, I was lacking the practical knowledge to keep them alive and healthy. Until I could find some information source or mentor, the logical thing to do was to observe them closely.

The kids snickered as they saw their mother stealthily approach the dove aviary, sidle alongside, and flatten against the wire like a B-movie spy. I can tell you plenty about the courting and mating habits of libidinous ringnecks; their pairings, spats, and consummations became my afternoon soap operas.

Ringneck males are hasty but considerate lovers; after mating, male and female doves tenderly groom each other by gently pulling at each other's neck feathers.

Since there would clearly be babies to deal with, I needed some expert advice—quickly—on welcoming a new generation. Also, I was concerned about the health of some of Eileen's doves. I was desperate for information, and the first phone call I made changed all our lives.

# THREE

# Bird Fever:
# One More Is No Big Deal

D oves are supposed to coo, but some of mine were hacking like congested old men. I needed a bird guru, and quickly. I had subscribed to the American Dove Association newsletter on the day Eileen handed it to me along with the six birds. When the first issue arrived, it included a membership directory of aviculturists. Louis Brown was a breeder whose species list was one of the longest and most exotic in the nation. He lived two hours from me. I called him.

"Yeah, this is Louis. What can I do for you? I'm kind of busy right now."

It was a small miracle that I got his sandpaper voice on the line. Louis doesn't answer his phone as a rule; he tends to view it as an instrument of torture on a par with thumbscrews. That day was an exception. He explained that he might have to hang up suddenly because he was expecting two important calls, one from a major zoo and the other from a fellow breeder. He was brokering a bird swap.

The call to Louis was my first exposure to the rare and idiosyncratic human specimens working in aviculture. The trade he was brokering was a triple play based on a complex system of avian chits. Louis explained that he would be sending a female Victoria crowned pigeon to a zoo that needed one. The zoo would be reclassifying a rare male African hornbill as "surplus" and sending it to a breeder who had a single female African hornbill in need of a mate. This breeder would in turn transfer two pairs of green-naped pheasant pigeons to Louis, who wanted them—badly. At the end of the day, the three parties would get what they needed, and no money would have exchanged hands.

Welcome to the bird bazaar, the type of arcane, sub-rosa marketplace that develops around cat fanciers, exotic-reptile breeders, and those besotted "orchid thieves" of book and film. Louis's level of high-stakes avian poker is fraught with feints, bluffs, and some undisguised pleading. The currency may include IOUs drawn on generations of rare birds yet unborn. Conservationists and collectors may have different motivations, but they all possess a certain crafty zeal for procuring what they desire. Louis described the acquisitive itch as "bird fever" and I hoped it wasn't catching. All I knew at the moment was that this guy was a master breeder. If zoos were vying for his birds, he must be able to help a humble backyard dove keeper. I'm sure that Louis could hear my anxiety over the line as I described the doves' persistent cough.

"Hoo boy, not good," Louis warned. "Could be contagious. Could be serious. Hard to fix. Should start treating 'em right away, nip the thing in the bud before all your birds get sick. I have some meds here that could work, but it's breeding season. I can't have you up here. I'll give you the phone number to order some. I'd show you how to give the pills, but nope, sorry . . . no one can come up when we're nesting here."

He described a marathon of round-the-clock vigilance overseeing the next crop of rare hatchlings. There were nest boxes to check, eggs to warm and "candle" (hold up to a light source) to see the activity within, and dozens of tiny, helpless babies to hand-feed with droppers and miniature shot glasses. Though disappointed, I was ready to say good-bye politely when I mentioned that we were headed toward his area to take our middle son, Jason, to camp.

"Holy cow, that camp is just down the road from me," Louis said. "I used to deliver hay there. Come on over."

I'd soon learn that Louis was as mercurial as he was kind. I decided to get up there before he changed his mind again. We left the two boys and Lizzy with a sitter. As we piled Jason, his camp gear, and a coffee cake for the Browns into the car for the drive north, I had no expectations beyond a quick stop for some information after the camp drop-off.

"Ten minutes, max," I promised Tom. How long could it take to learn to dose a dove?

. . .

THE BROWNS LIVE at the end of a quiet street in a semirural area an hour northeast of San Francisco. Their grounds are concealed by tall pampas grass along the perimeter. Peek over the chain-link gate across the driveway and you get the first clue that the small, weathered ranch house is no ordinary home. There are geese and pheasants in the front yard, and the entire garden is netted.

Carol met us at the door dressed in jeans and a turtleneck— her basic uniform, I'd later learn. She struck me as a leaner version of Mrs. Santa Claus, with short wavy silver hair, soft eyes, and the most genuine of smiles. Louis stood behind her in overalls, an old T-shirt, and the sort of wide black safety belt worn by weight lifters. His hair was long; his stubble, some days old. Caring for over a thousand birds is dirty, heavy work, and the years have taken a toll: Louis has a litany of ailments, and Carol leans on a cane to favor what she calls "this darn hip." For me, it was as fateful a moment as cradling the dove on the highway—but with much happier results. I had just met my teachers, confessors, procurers, and dear friends for life.

"You're gonna see birds that will knock your socks off," Louis announced.

He led Tom and me through a heavy metal door that clanged shut behind us. We both gasped. It was like the moment Dorothy steps out of Auntie Em's house in Oz and the scene changes suddenly to dazzling color. For over two hours, we ogled the Browns' sublime creatures as they went about their day, strutting, flapping, roosting, nesting, preening. The aviaries themselves were the plainest of settings for the jewel-toned treasures within. Louis is a frugal, practical sort, who "makes do" with bits of wire, corrugated metal roofing, rewired incubators, and repurposed orange crates. Magnificent Chinese golden pheasants with deep orange capes fairly glowed through pedestrian chicken wire. The effect was part Xanadu, part Dogpatch. We were utterly entranced.

We followed Louis down an aisle beneath rows of skylights. There were antic, meowing owl finches and chartreuse Guinea turacos from Africa, emerald doves and plum-headed parakeets from India. The bleeding-heart doves from the Philippines looked dramatically wounded with a convincing splotch of red feathers midbreast. We moved on to Australian crested doves, lorikeets, and rosellas from Australia. They ranged in size from two-inch finches to pheasants with five-foot tails. I nearly swooned when a dun-colored gray peacock-pheasant greeted Louis's approach by spreading its tail into an upright fan studded with circular patterns that glowed iridescent, like so many metallic eyes, blazing as the sun touched them.

Wandering the labyrinth with its devoted guardian was a deeper, far more intimate experience than seeing exotic animals in a zoo. I tried my best to remember the names of the birds as Louis pointed them out, but I gave up, overwhelmed. Tom always carries a stack of three-by-five cards and a pen with him. He jotted down names and circled those he found especially beautiful. As a painter, Tom is drawn to bold, saturated, natural color. I noticed him lingering at the aviary full of scarlet-chested grass parakeets. It's easy to see why they're also called splendid parrots. The males are splashed with dense primary colors: green head, blue back, red chest, and yellow underbelly.

There was one bird that we had heard but not seen. We were intrigued by its call, which was a loud, low-pitched booming. We asked Louis what could make such a sound. "Victoria crowned pigeons. World's largest pigeon. Dodo used to be—now these birds have the crown." He chuckled at his pun and led the way to yet another cabinet of wonders. The Victoria crowned pigeons were among his greatest loves, ever since he first saw one at another breeder's home nearby.

"That's the first kind of bird I got goofy over," he admitted. "I couldn't get it out of my head. I just had to find some for myself." "Getting goofy," I'd learn too well, was to fall in thrall so deeply with a species that you'll extend your search over years, miles, and continents. How many times since then have I pulled up to an airport cargo area and listened anxiously for the sound of scratching from a small plastic carrier? Catching bird fever could get mighty expensive, Louis warned. A healthy Victoria crowned pair capable of reproducing "could run you five grand." When we finally did see the big boomers, they trotted up to Louis for a pet or a scratch.

"Big babies," he growled. So trusting and unafraid of humans that they were easily trapped or slaughtered in the New Guinea wild.

TWO HOURS LATER, we sat down to coffee with the Browns. Over the afternoon, we had come to realize that theirs is a deep, organic partnership, with Louis handling the aviaries and commerce and Carol managing the delicate art of incubating and hand-raising the rare babies. The kitchen is the heart of their operation, cluttered with baskets full of magnificent feathers and bowls of hollowed eggshells in speckles, blue greens, and deep purples. Fruit bowls share counter space with old incubator parts. Though Louis's obsession started with a single African gray parrot that he still has, he and Carol now raise over a hundred species, some of which they sell to zoos and to a short list of wealthy collectors. Like the farmers in the surrounding area, they work from sunup to sundown, every single day. Their aviaries don't have a name, they don't advertise or attend conventions, and they're not on the Internet. I don't think they even have a cell phone. Not surprisingly, Louis's grown children have no interest in this demanding family trade. Carol and Louis have not left their birds for a vacation in over forty years.

Bird experts and enthusiasts—ornithologists, zookeepers, collectors, artists—come to *them*. An East Coast Amish breeder once hired a driver to take him all the way across the country to see the Browns so that he could "happen to be in the neighborhood" and wangle an invitation to see their birds. If you have been in an American zoo or a theme park with exotic-bird exhibits, chances are you've seen birds that were raised by Louis and Carol.

In terms of breeding rare birds, Louis's closest competitor may be a Qatari billionaire, Sheikh Saoud bin Mohammed bin Ali al-Thani. On a preserve nearly two square miles on the Arabian Peninsula, the sheikh has rescued the Brazilian Spix's macaw from certain extinction. His facility keeps two thousand rare and endangered animals from over ninety species—including green-naped pheasant pigeons. The sheikh has a staff of two hundred, including four vets and five biologists. Louis and Carol have Hector, a compassionate, dedicated gentleman who shoulders fifty-pound sacks of seed and patrols the perimeter for rats, coons, and coyotes.

The Browns' specialty is hard-to-breed birds in the Columbidae family. They are legendary for puzzling out what precise conditions a species needs in order to reproduce. In the decade since my first visit that day, Carol has been a patient and knowing midwife to plenty of my hatchlings, via phone.

Like a world-class collector chasing that illusive Picasso etching or first-issue stamp, Louis was challenged—and a bit irked—by his failures with green-naped pheasant pigeons. They were about the only dove species that he had not successfully bred yet. He was pleased to have made that three-way trade so that he could try again with new pairs. He once had three pairs of green-napeds, but none produced any young. Back then, Louis was working full-time as a butcher, buying and selling real estate on the side, and raising birds as a hobby. Once he retired and could devote all his time to the birds, he was confident he could find the secret to breeding these delicate, fragile birds.

Should they discover the key to producing healthy hatchlings, he and Carol would not keep that information to themselves. This kind, unpretentious pair is unique in the bird-breeding world because they share knowledge and open their aviaries to fellow breeders. I didn't realize it then, but I would be dealing with a fairly closed brotherhood. Most other breeders—nearly all are men—are extremely secretive and rarely allow anyone to see their birds or their facilities.

Louis left the kitchen to net and prepare some birds for travel. I was amazed—and amused—to see my budget-conscious husband become enthralled enough about a couple of Louis's species to buy some. Having Tom there with me was a very good thing. If I had tried to describe the wonders I saw that day, he would never have believed me. It has to be easier to live with the obsessed when you've entered the holy of holies as well. Maybe . . .

We got set to leave the Browns' with a pair of those irresistible scarlet-chested grass parakeets and a pair of Australian crested doves—Tom's purchases. Louis gifted us with a male African half-collared dove, three Senegal doves, and an emerald dove missing a foot. As we loaded up, Tom turned to Louis and asked casually, "We can put these guys together in one aviary, right?"

"No way! Got to keep the parakeets and doves separate, since psittacines [parrots and parakeets] dehusk their seed while doves eat the seed whole. And those Australian crested doves, keep them by themselves. Buggers can be aggressive when they're nesting. You can put the half-collared with your ringnecks, but I wouldn't. They can crossbreed. Same issue with the Senegal doves."

On the drive home, Tom was uncharacteristically quiet. With the day's additions, our avian population had almost doubled from twelve birds and two species (six doves and six chickens) to twenty-one birds and seven species. Apparently we'd need three more aviaries; one for the grass parakeets, one for the Australian crested doves, one for the half-collared. And where could we safely house the handicapped emerald dove? On we drove, with a backseat full of noisy gifts and impulse buys and an uneasy silence between us.

I was still concerned about my ability to care for new species. When I mused aloud about making more trips to the Browns' for instruction, Tom was worried that I'd bring back more than information. After all, he had fallen hard for those birds himself. "Honey, why don't you volunteer at a humane society that takes in wild birds?" he suggested sweetly. "That way you'll learn about birds while you're helping out."

We hired a carpenter to build a freestanding aviary. He normally worked for an orchid grower, building greenhouses. His aviary was spectacular, a seven-foot hexagon with a shingled roof. The sides were wire with fitted Plexiglas panels that could

Coffee, *Victoria crowned pigeon*

Amadeus, *Lady Ross's turaco*

Amigo, *red-headed Amazon parrot*

Shana, *yellow-naped Amazon parrot*

Tico, *blue and gold macaw*

*Crimson wing parrot*

*Lady Gouldian finch*

*Turaco*

Lancelot, *green-naped pheasant pigeon*

*Australian crested dove*

*Bleeding-heart dove*

*Ringneck dove*

be removed in the heat of the summer but easily put back to protect from drafts in the winter. The structure was so handsome that a local newspaper ran an article with a photo of it in late 2001. As I delved deeper into the science of bird keeping, I realized that much of the construction was all wrong for keeping the floor clean or making the birds feel secure. But it sure looked great.

We named it the Aussie Aviary and moved the scarlet-chested grass parakeets into it. They thrived; within two years our pair would become fourteen. We had divided the aviary into separate sections and an annex for the other birds. Then the ringnecks had babies; so did the Australian crested. In the crowded conditions, turf wars erupted. It was time for another aviary. And so it went.

# FOUR

# Do You Speak Bird?

A grocery clerk was straightening up the produce section when he noticed a small paper bag atop a mound of celery. A few hours later, the bag was still there. He opened it, expecting to find and restock a shopper's forgotten vegetables. Instead, a live bird stared up at him. He was tiny, with a body about the size of a Ping-Pong ball. His feathers were light brown with chocolate-toned streaks down his back.

This was a coturnix Japanese quail, and in all likelihood the shopper who forgot the bag was probably browsing for some spring onions to sauté along with the bird. A more serious gourmand would have consumed him as a few crunchy bites glazed in a bourbon-jalapeño reduction. Coturnix quail are some gourmets' delight, raised commercially for their delicate dark flesh and their eggs. The Internet is brimming with health claims for the inch-and-a-half-long brown speckled eggs; they are touted as balms for everything from inflammatory diseases to erectile dysfunction. Quail eggs are used in facial masks and hair care products and hailed for their quotients of antioxidants, essential fatty oils, thiamine, and riboflavin.

This "farmed" quail had likely been bought at a live-animal market that morning. The bird peered up at the startled grocery clerk and let out a high-pitched squeal. To a first-time listener, quail song sounds like that of an oversize cricket. Listen to a coturnix closely enough and the lilting, upper-register notes are evocative of a violin or viola. The song is quite moving and beautiful.

Six hundred years ago in feudal Japan, this little ball of feathers in a paper sack might have been worth his weight in captured silver—prized for his artistry, rather than his flesh. Samurai warriors were among those who kept these quail as songbirds. Contests were held to judge the most beautiful performance. Much later, some breeders practiced photostimulation, manipulating artificial light to get the birds to sing in winter. The coturnix's transformation from diva to dinner course arrived around the turn of the twentieth century; legend has it that the Japanese emperor ate these quail as a cure for his tuberculosis. The species was eventually imported and domesticated in the United States.

The quail in this supermarket was lucky on three counts. First, he was forgotten by the person intending to eat him, and then he was given to a local humane society. Had the clerk turned him loose in the nearest field, he would never have survived in the wild. The shelter that accepted him had a well-regarded wildlife rehabilitation center, and that was the quail's third bit of luck: during the intake process, a clerk misclassified the bird as "wildlife" in the computer system instead of the more accurate designation of "farm animal."

This was a reprieve from being sent to the nearest quail farm and back to market. But it landed him in a confusing thicket of human bureaucracy. Birds designated wildlife are never offered for adoption. Unless they are permanently injured, they are rereleased into the wild. This bird was not listed as native American wildlife, given his species origin in Japan. Bottom line: the staff could not release the quail because he wasn't native, but they couldn't put him up for adoption either.

The coturnix stayed at the humane society for several months, marooned in a clerical catch-22. A kennel assistant there noticed the quail and offered to adopt or buy him for a light supper. The adoption counselor who reviewed the application was concerned. Humane societies are not in the business of placing animals so that they can be eaten. She declined the "adoption," and soon afterward I heard from her.

"I looked up his paperwork and realized the mistake in his classification," the adoption counselor told me. "Then I decided to call you. This bird needs to be in a sanctuary where he will be safe. He is absolutely adorable. You'll love him."

Great, I thought. Another learning curve, and another expense. Tom's suggestion that I do volunteer work in local bird shelters had been a good one, but I'm afraid its effect had been the opposite of what he'd intended in seeking to curb our ever-growing bird population. I loved the work and learned a lot about how to identify, handle, feed, and medicate birds. Tom knew that wild birds were not eligible for adoption. There was another department at the humane society, however, that put pet birds up for adoption, and now I was called pretty regularly. We had more birds than ever.

I had no experience with quail and I was reluctant to add another species to the diverse group already housed in our backyard. The counselor persuaded me that the quail would be very easy to keep. She had placed other birds with us, including an Indian ringneck parrot and a pair of rosy Bourkes, pretty little pink-and-blue parakeets with sweet dispositions. She had campaigned very hard for a cockatoo named Angel, but I came to my senses and declined. Despite that single rational no, the counselor knew the buttons to push.

"He's the size of a baby chick, he's very friendly, he's loved by everyone on the staff. He is really a darling. Trust me, you won't regret taking him."

She was right; we all fell for him. For his part, the little quail bestowed a huge gift: he taught me the rudiments of how to speak bird.

I CALLED HIM Sweetie, because he was just that. When I set him into our smallest five-by-seven-foot aviary—which was far larger than his cage at the shelter—he raced excitedly around its perimeter, scuttled back to me, and burst into song. Anytime I went to feed him, he'd react the same way. When he noticed me at the aviary door, he would leave off with whatever he was doing—pecking at a meal or giving himself a dust bath—and race toward me. If I sat down on the aviary floor, Sweetie would jump into my lap. If I stroked his head, he would sing.

I could see how he might have bewitched even a battle-toughened samurai warrior. Before long, I was familiar enough with his repertoire of songs to hear nuances in rhythm and pitch. Sweetie seemed to crave human company, especially mine. When I came anywhere near his aviary, he'd run to the wire and look expectant. I was besotted, yet I was also wary when I went into his cage. He was so tame that he was always darting swiftly underfoot, and his coloring blended in with the aviary floor. I was worried that one of us might step on him. I hung a caution sign on his cage to remind everyone to be very careful.

One day I heard Tom laughing from behind Sweetie's aviary. When I went over to see what had tickled him so, he pointed to two of our oldest son's friends, who were walking back toward the house. They were big boys, with linebacker physiques. Tom replayed their conversation for me.

"The thing must be poisonous."

"Maybe it does something like leap up and peck your eyes out."

"I dare you to walk in there."

"No way. You first."

Tom had gone over to chat them up and make sure there were no intrusions into Sweetie's territory. He was still laughing once they had disappeared into the house. "They were afraid of that tiny quail!"

"But why?"

I was mystified. Then Tom pointed to my sign and started laughing again. I guess my hastily scrawled warning was open to interpretation. On a board three feet square in huge letters I'd written: DANGER! DON'T ENTER!

IT MAY HAVE been ludicrous to imagine Sweetie as an attack quail, but I can say that his charm was a sweet sort of tyranny. When he ran to me, I had to put other bird chores on hold to enjoy this tiny bird with the outsize personality. I learned to feed him last so as not to be late in getting to birds scheduled after him. The reason was simple. When he sat in my lap and sang, I lost track of time.

Like any virtuoso, Sweetie had very strong preferences, especially when it came to food. When I brought him home from the shelter, I fed him game-bird mash, as recommended by the humane society. The food is protein rich, formulated to supply all needed minerals and vitamins for game birds. Since quail are considered game birds, the choice of food seemed reasonable.

Our pheasants, also game birds, loved chopped-up greens, so I offered him these, as well as "birdie bread," a homemade corn bread with strained baby-food veggies, eggs (including the shells), shredded carrots, and pellets in it. Most of our birds reacted to it as a yummy treat.

Not Sweetie. I would enter his aviary carrying food dishes, and he would run to me and watch intently as I put them down. He poked his beak into each dish and then turned his gaze upward. I kept trying: crushed Cheerios, fruit cut into tiny pieces, bread crumbs, hard-boiled eggs mashed into a paste. The reaction was the same, yet I could tell he was hungry. He'd look at me as if to say, Why can't you understand what I want? and then he'd let out a soft cry like a trill.

"Eek!"

I've reproduced it as best I can given the limits of our alphabet.

Likely translation: Seriously? Human, you disappoint me again. And I'm hungry.

When Sweetie's adoption counselor called to check in, I voiced my frustration with our picky eater. "I'm sorry. I should have told you," she apologized. "He absolutely adores mealworms. We gave him three or four of them every day."

That afternoon I bought my first batch of mealworms. When I presented the first worm to Sweetie, he was so excited he tried to leap up to my fingers to claim him prize. He gobbled up all four worms that I'd placed on the ground for him. I sat down and gave Sweetie a boost up into my lap. As I stroked his head and listened to his postprandial trill, I felt as buoyant as he sounded.

All was rosy between us until a shipment of mealworms was late to my vendor. Standing disconsolately over my substitution, Sweetie let me have it.

"*EEK! EEK! EEK!*"

Chastened, I searched all over and found another source that had some in stock. The clerk asked me if I wanted to have the worms coated in vitamins. It had never occurred to me to do this, but I realized it was a good idea. After that, I used worms as a delivery system for powdered vitamins and any necessary medications for many other birds. Score another lesson for Sweetie. This was a procedural advance, but the bigger lesson I was about to learn was this: listen hard enough and you'll realize that a bird can communicate with humans, and in more than one way.

Sweetie was so expressive and so clearly interested in engaging me that I was determined that we try to learn each other's language. He had already taken the first step with consistently using the same "eek" sound to communicate that he wanted worms. I decided I would test out my first word in bird. I went to Sweetie's aviary with the package of worms hidden in my pocket.

"Eek," I told him as best I could.

No response.

"*EEK*"? "Eek"? "*EEEEEK*"? I dangled a worm from my fingers.

I wasn't able to even come close to the exact sound he used, but when he saw the worm I was holding, he ran up to me, stood at my feet, and looked up expectantly.

"Eek," he said.

"Eek," I responded. Finally, success! He began jumping up the same way he did upon seeing a worm in my hand. I took the container of mealworms out, dumped a bunch on the ground, and let him have a feast. I practiced all day. "Eek. Eek. Eek. Eek." The sound was imprecise, but I wanted to be consistent at least and make the same sound each time.

Tom thought I was losing my mind. The children made it clear they agreed. They just hoped that none of their pals were around at feeding time. How might it look to see someone's mom squatting in a cage, croaking? I had a rejoinder for their teasing.

"Keep it up and you get 'eek' for supper."

From then on, when I croaked my "eek," Sweetie knew that it meant a worm was coming. I realized that if I wanted to communicate further with Sweetie, not only did I have to use the same verbal cues, but I also had to become far more consistent in my use of body language. Any thought or desire had to be represented by one sound, one gesture—with just one meaning.

Over time, Sweetie responded to almost a dozen words or gestures. I felt as if I understood at least as many parts of his language, spoken or behavioral. There was a certain way that he approached me if he wanted to be picked up, another if he didn't. He'd let me know if he liked something by a particular purr. And of course, if I didn't produce "eek" when he wanted it, I'd have one unhappy quail.

I began to use the same principles—observation, consistency, and attention to detail—to try to communicate with other birds. Through experimentation with what worked and what didn't, I've learned that if I'm patient and alert, the bird will let me know what it wants. Though none of our wild birds were as receptive to humans as Sweetie, many showed the inclination to communicate. Even wild birds not given to being social toward humans expressed their needs, their problems, and their state of well-being in sounds and behavior that were perfectly intelligible—as long as I paid attention.

Looking hard was as essential as listening. Birds do use clear, easy-to-understand, and consistent signals to communicate with us. Most seasoned aviculturists can tell from the aviary commotion or the change in calls when their birds are alarmed, fighting among themselves, mourning, or content. We have learned to identify begging movements, courting dances, and the body language that warns us to stay away from a nest. Even pet owners with a single bird quickly learn to identify what we might classify as a state of mind. If you have an Amazon parrot, it would be a painful mistake to ignore the low body stance, open beak, and dilated eyes of a bird that's not in the mood to be handled.

Desperate situations can compel otherwise uncommunicative birds to alert humans who might help. One day I was puzzled at the flight pattern of a male crested quail-dove, a luminescent dove from the same island hills that produce Jamaica Blue Mountain coffee. He flew back and forth from a planter inside the aviary. I realized that he wanted me to focus my attention on it. When I looked behind it, there was a newly fledged baby wedged between the planter and the wall. A rescue was effected, and all was well.

Birds are emphatic food critics. Should we feed them seeds too large, they will dump them all out on the ground and eat only the small ones. A piece of fruit or vegetable too bulky to manipulate is repeatedly picked up and dropped until a clueless human gets the message.

I don't whistle well, which can be a handicap for an aviculturist. Accomplished ornithologists can imitate a species' call in the wild and get an instant response. Instead of complicated whistles, I decided to continue to use basic, monosyllabic English words—consistently, and with close attention to my own body language. I did add a series of simple whistles with very clear meanings. The most useful has been my netting whistle. Netting birds for transfer or medical checks is necessary but stressful. If I must net a bird, I enter the aviary straightforwardly, with a net in hand and clearly visible. I never pretend to be bringing food or a treat. I use a particular whistle to broadcast my intention to net, and I never use that sound in any other situation. I stare at the bird to be netted, and I'm very careful not to look at any other bird inside.

Sometimes, the birds are complicit. Cabernet was a crimson rosella who tended to bully the other inhabitants of his aviary, which has a soaring twenty-foot ceiling. He needed to be moved, but the height would make it difficult. If it took a long time to net him, other birds might panic and get hurt by flying into walls, perches, or one another. I walked into the aviary and stared only at Cabernet. The other birds stayed calm and moved quietly out of the way as I chased my quarry. When I finally cornered him and got him in the net, the other birds seemed perfectly calm. It may be my imagination that they were pleased to be rid of the bully boy. What I am sure of is that the netting method has proved to be effective body language that reassures the other birds: Hey, it's not about you. And nobody gets hurt.

There are also simple ways of assuring wild birds that it's okay when a well-intentioned human intrudes. By now, both birds and humans at Pandemonium are used to the "Michele crouch," my preferred posture for entering an aviary to do routine maintenance, water a plant, or check a food bowl. The birds have come to understand that if I hold my body low, they can go about their business without interference. This has greatly reduced panic flying, which can cause injuries and needless stress.

So much changed for the better once I realized that birds are close and shrewd observers of human behavior. As I engaged them in a consistent and repetitive form of communication, a new dimension of my relationship with them opened. I hate to think what I might have missed were it not for Sweetie, our foundling from the produce department.

Given what the quail taught me, I would have been a block-head not to realize that despite his excitement at seeing me every day, the company of his own kind would be far more enriching. We added more coturnix quail, and I think that Sweetie was a pretty content bird. His was an active, song-filled aviary when I brought my friend Janie by to look at all the birds. She was an accomplished cook who had fed Tom and me some fabulous meals. Janie stopped and stared fixedly at the sight of Sweetie.

"Yum," she said.

I took her elbow and steered her toward some decidedly un-appetizing grass parakeets. "Remind me," I told her, as lightly as I could, "never to ask you to house-sit."

# FIVE

# It Was Raining Birds

Without realizing it, I had become one of those women—an otherwise reasonable adult whose growing passion for a certain kind of living thing, be it potbellied pigs or Pomeranians, causes a certain amount of eye rolling and outright pity for those who love and live with her. Yes, I was a Bird Lady. I watched friends' eyes glaze over at one too many birdie tales. Even good girlfriends stopped calling when I had canceled too many hikes, lunches, or shopping trips in favor of treks to the feed and grain store or an intense session of deworming. Most afternoons after a long day in the aviaries, work clothes spattered with bird poop and hands reeking of disinfectant, I was no fit sight for the designer floor of Neiman Marcus in rubber clogs.

But I was never lonesome, and there was real meaning to my madness. Calls came in from sanctuaries, rescue groups, and panicky individuals who heard that a woman up in Los Altos was a sucker for unwanted birds. Our answering machine was full of offers that were hard to refuse.

"I've lost my job and my home. There are two cockatiels . . ."

"Heard you take birds that need a home. Listen, if you'll pay the shipping . . ."

"My breast cancer has come back. I'm starting four weeks of chemo. Please, take my bird."

My guidelines were simple. I turned down the best and the brightest in favor of the most unwanted. Birds that talked, had no behavioral problems, and were beautiful, easy to keep, and in good shape, I politely declined to take. I figured that birds like these would easily find a home. But handicapped birds that were old, sick, or in need of specialized food or housing—birds at risk—I did my best to accept. I felt I was in control of my own compulsions: I was no collector of rare, beautiful things but a rescuer of lost, damaged, or unloved birds.

In they fluttered—pheasants, lovebirds, more dove species. Within a year of meeting the Browns in 2001, our backyard population grew exponentially: 33 birds by the end of 2002, 68 in 2003, and 119—representing thirty-three species—by the end of 2004.

FROM THE LATE 1990s until around 2010, it was raining birds. I wish I had understood the reason why at the time. Avid watchers of wild birds scan the Weather Channel for storm systems that "drop" thousands of migrating birds—a bounty of viewable species—down into an area to ride out the weather. I had stumbled onto the scene in the midst of a huge upheaval in American aviculture. It wasn't weather in-duced. The huge changes were the result of legislation enacted in 1992 that was good for wild birds but hugely problematic for commercial breeders and private collectors. For a rescue opera-tion like mine, it opened the floodgates. Briefly, this is what happened.

Before 1992, over three hundred thousand birds were taken yearly from wild forests, savannas, and marshes around the world for import to America—chiefly for the pet trade. Some of these birds were stolen directly from their nests. A standard method of reaching the nest was to cut down the tree that housed it. This procedure delivered a deadly one-two punch to wild bird populations. Nestlings were taken—along with their contributions to future generations—and their nesting areas were destroyed. Habitat destruction became more and more of an issue as forests were cut down for lumber or human develop-ment. Traps using live birds as decoys were also used, along with snares made of fishing line. Birds were caught en masse in "mist nets," which are large, thin nylon nets, set up somewhat like volleyball nets, that capture anything that flies in. In the hands of trained, certified users, mist nets have proved to be an effective means of trapping birds for banding and scientific study without injury. Deployed by profit-minded commercial trappers, they can be deadly catchalls.

The collateral damage was appalling: for every live bird that made it into pet stores and people's homes, it is estimated that three birds died either during seizure, in transit, or in quarantine. Needless to say, taking a million birds year after year from the wild was not good for birds or the planet. The Wild Bird Conservation Act of 1992 limited importation of birds to two companion birds per year and required extensive documentation to prove that the birds were indeed pets, not captured wildlife intended for sale. The effect of the law on the numbers of birds imported into the United States was immediate and dramatic. In 1993, the year the law took effect, the number of birds imported fell to fewer than three thousand.

If bird breeders here understood the need for such protection, they were unprepared for the profound effect on their operations. Before 1992, they were able to breed a large variety of birds. If they lost a bird or needed new blood, they could get what they needed by buying or trading for a wild-caught bird. The ready source of new genetic material meant that breeding stocks could be kept vibrant. Without the wild as a source of birds, there was no option other than to breed birds already in the United States. However, some species breed more easily and are more marketable than others. Parrots were at the top of the list in each category. Our aviaries would feel the effects of the resulting parrot "glut" a bit later on.

The strategy that most breeders adopted was to specialize in raising pet birds on either end of the price spectrum: the very expensive birds like parrots, macaws, and cockatoos, or the "mass produced" small birds like budgies and finches. Birds that didn't fit into these categories were discarded. Doves and pigeons did not make it onto the "hot" list.

I sure did have a lot of them. From my inexperienced vantage point, the supply of birds seemed inexhaustible. Now I know that just the opposite was true. Yes, there were a lot of exotic doves and pigeons available for free or for bargain-basement prices, but that was not, as I assumed, normal. Breeders and collectors who realized the limitations of the new law wanted no part of species that, like discontinued china patterns, would be impossible to replenish should any of the pieces be lost.

THROUGHOUT THIS PERIOD, as I continued accepting birds in need of homes, my network of sources somehow grew to include rescue groups, humane societies, and veterinarians. In addition, I met a lot of people with far worse cases of bird fever when Louis and Carol Brown invited me to the aviculturists' ultimate ball—their annual Christmas party. It was the same deal every year: Elite breeders in overalls and steel-tipped work boots dropped their wives' potluck dishes on a groaning table and sidled off to talk birds. The women spoke of grandchildren; the men stood in tight clusters discussing mealworms and roost disinfectant. At first, no men talked to me, until I met Larry, who also seemed a bit ill at ease, or just bored. Larry's partner, Justin, was the bigger bird enthusiast, and he was off in a corner swapping yarns. Larry and I fell into deep conversation, and over the course of the next year, the three of us became long-distance bird pals, trading tips and gossip.

Justin and Larry lived south in San Diego, where they kept a meticulously curated collection of exotic birds. Then they broke up. Their settlement divided the birds between them. Justin kept his, but Larry wasn't keen on having these living, demanding reminders of a lost love. One day I found a message from him on my answering machine: "Expect some birds to come through the US post office. If you can breed these guys, the other bird breeders will be eating out of your hands and begging to talk to you at the next Christmas party. Hang in there."

The following day, the phone rang at 6:15 a.m. It was an anxious-sounding postal worker. "We have three crates of live birds for you. We'd appreciate if you could come right down to pick them up."

"Are you open this early?" I asked.

"Not generally to the public, but we like to get live animals out of here ASAP. Come to the loading dock. Ask anyone you see there for the birds that just came in. We took a peek to check their condition, and no one here has ever seen anything like them. What kind are they?"

I told him I hadn't the slightest idea.

I was getting used to such surprises. Birds were arriving

unbidden, unannounced, and sometimes anonymously, like the pair of very rare crested quail-doves, native to Jamaica, that had turned up earlier that week in an unmarked box. When I got Larry's crates home, my hands shook a bit as I opened each one.

The first box held a single turaco. "*Whoo, whoo, whooo,*" she yelled when I looked in the crate. According to the accompanying paperwork, the bird was a female Guinea turaco. Her smooth, short bright green feathers ended in a zany crested tuft on her head. She peered at me through startling red-and-white eye markings and opened her orange beak again: "*WHOOOOO.*" Despite her long boxed journey, this was a gal with personality to spare.

The second box had a pair of Nicobar pigeons, which I'd admired at the Browns'. Nicobar pigeons are black, crow-size birds that look somewhat sinister in the shade but whose feathers glow blue green in sunlight. They have a fringe of feathers that stick out around their neck like the top of a court jester's jacket.

The final box held a pair of odd-looking birds. They looked like an afterthought, put together with parts from several species. They had football-shaped bodies, and beaks that seemed more appropriate to a duck. Red lines streaked their yellow legs; it appeared as though they had varicose veins. When I called Louis to describe the birds to him, he got pretty excited.

"You don't know what you have there."

They were the species Louis was so intent on breeding, the green-naped pheasant pigeons. His words turned out to be a huge understatement. The two green-napeds would live quietly in their own aviary for a few years until a sad event there changed the whole trajectory of Pandemonium and my journey in aviculture. But that day when all the birds arrived, my main concern was how to explain the population increase to my family.

"I had nothing to do with this!" I swore to Tom when he arrived home that night and gaped at the assortment of new arrivals. It just might be time to surprise him with a pair of the miniature donkeys I'd seen for sale at a farm near the Browns'. Sometimes the best defense is offense. But where would I fit a corral?

# SIX

# Amigo: A Bird and His Boy

Another dove seemed ill, and I gently put it in a small dog carrier for a trip to the vet. As a novice bird keeper, I had come to rely on Dr. Varner for her avian expertise and advice. Our youngest son, Nick, then twelve, was with me as I sat in the waiting room. He had come to the clinic with me a few times before and knew his way around, so I let him go off to the restroom alone. A short time later, he joined me in the examining room, where a vet tech was weighing the dove. The tech and I looked up, startled.

Nick had a small parrot on his shoulder. This one was a beauty, about ten inches high, with green feathers and a vibrant red head. The bird was tenderly preening Nick's hair. My smiling boy was stroking the parrot's neck and head.

"Look, Mom, I have a new bird. He likes me. Can I take him home?"

The vet tech paled. She put the dove back in its carrier and tore out of the room in search of Dr. Varner. I just stared.

The boy and the bird looked adorable together, but I quickly launched into every mom's "not so fast" speech.

"No, we can't take a strange parrot home, even if we wanted a parrot. Which we don't. Besides, if it's here at the vet's, it must have an owner. You should know better than to touch someone else's bird without permission."

Nick had a story ready. He insisted that he hadn't done anything wrong. He claimed that the parrot was the instigator; it had picked the lock on its cage, opened the door, and hopped onto Nick's shoulder.

Right.

"He likes me and he wants to come home with me."

That tore it.

"You expect me to believe he's talking to you as well? No way you're taking this or any other parrot home."

Nick invoked the recent death of his beloved companion, a sweet golden retriever named Sandy. She had been by Nick's side all his life. When we had discussed getting another dog, Nick was adamant: He didn't want one. Never, ever again. Until that moment in the clinic, he hadn't mentioned Sandy at all in the few months since her death. Clearly I was mistaken in thinking he had worked through his grief. Maternal guilt began to melt my resolve. Maybe a parrot wasn't a bad pet for a growing boy; I'd heard that these birds can live for decades, so it wouldn't be likely to die anytime soon. This tame, attentive little bird seemed drawn to our son. It was very tender in its grooming, running its beak down a strand of Nick's longish light brown hair, cocking its head to look up at Nick's face.

My soft-focus reverie dissolved as Dr. Varner rushed into the room with three vet techs. One held a towel, another a large stick, the third a net. Dr. Varner had a tranquilizer syringe. She spoke to the bird in a firm voice charged with concern: "Step off, Amigo!"

The parrot ignored both her command and the stick that a vet tech was holding out as a perch. Dr. Varner appealed to Nick: "Slowly and carefully, step toward the table so he can hop off there."

"Why? He doesn't want to get off and I don't want him to either."

I was mortified by his defiance and snapped, "Nick, listen to Dr. Varner. You should not have touched that bird."

He stuck to his story that it was all Amigo's doing, and he repeated the tale for the doctor—with embellishments.

"He kept yelling, 'Hello, hello,' at me, so I went to his cage. But I didn't touch anything. He was the one who opened the door and climbed on my shoulder—didn't you, bud?"

Amigo burbled back some parrotspeak, and Nick swore he understood.

"He says he wants to come home with me."

The darn bird was nodding his head. Dr. Varner flinched as he stretched his neck toward Nick's face and bellowed, "Amigo!

Amigo! Amigo!" Then he maneuvered his beak very close to Nick's ear and spoke into it, loudly and clearly: "I love you!"

Here's where the music should have swelled up, boy and bird nuzzling as they walk off into a Technicolor happy ending. In fact, one vet tech was wiping her eyes. Another sighed. Dr. Varner had been quiet for a moment, as if in deep thought. When she spoke again, her voice had a tinge of relief: "Amigo does need a home, Nick. If it's okay with your mom, he can go home with you."

What? It was time for a consultation beyond earshot of boy and bird. Before we left the room, Dr. Varner addressed Nick firmly. "Your mother and I will talk about what is going to happen next, but not while Amigo is on your shoulder. Stand next to the exam table and let him step off." They both complied right away. As we left the room, the techs stayed and stood sentinel, chatting with Nick about what Amigo liked to eat.

"Amigo is an Amazon parrot," Dr. Varner explained once she had closed the door. "With Amazons, it's not a question of whether, but when, they will bite."

My stomach constricted as I pictured the sharp, hooked beak grooming Nick's hair. It was an easy reach from Nick's shoulder for Amigo to extract a chunk of cheek—or an eye. Nick must have been too short at the time to see the sign atop the bird's cage. It bore a crudely drawn skull and crossbones and the warning, DON'T TOUCH. PARROT BITES. If this was indeed a vicious attack parrot, what explained his behavior toward Nick?

And why on earth would a talented, responsible vet suggest we take such a creature home?

Dr. Varner said that she would tell me as much as she knew about Amigo before I made a decision. First, she exonerated my son: "I wouldn't be surprised if Nick's story is true. I didn't figure Amigo for being a lock picker. He's never tried it before, but some of the other parrots who have been here for a while have been masterly at finding ways to get out of their cages."

Okay, he's smart, observant, and deft as a cat burglar. But about the biting . . . was there a long pattern of it?

"Amigo is at least twenty-seven years old," Dr. Varner went on. "All I know of his history is that he had been placed in a bad home after being rescued from an even worse one."

Parrots change owners so often that there is a word for it: *rehoming.* Dr. Varner pointed out that moving between homes was not in itself indicative of a character flaw in the bird; generally the failing is human. Parrots are not easy pets, and people often buy them unaware of what they're taking on. According to the Humane Society of the United States, the average pet parrot goes through numerous homes just in the first decade of its life. Dr. Varner ventured, "I wouldn't be surprised if Amigo had a lot more than average."

When Amigo had arrived at her clinic with his latest owner, the parrot was very ill and overweight. In fact, he was a fat guy. Overfeeding is a common problem with parrots that get little exercise and are often fed seed diets more calorie-rich than the fruits and berries they would have eaten in the wild. Treats such as sunflower seeds and peanuts are also high in fat. Parrot obesity can cause serious health problems, including fatty tumors and a potentially fatal condition known as hepatic lipidosis, when so much fat is stored in the liver that it can cease to function. It's distressingly easy to love an exotic bird to death.

In the years since Dr. Varner first explained Amigo's weight issues—and as our own flock of parrot adoptees grew—I've heard other veterinarians voice frustration with this syndrome. One told me, "Over and over, I'd wonder why a twenty-five-year-old parrot would die of heart disease. They should be living twice that long. Then a necropsy would reveal completely clogged arteries. People may love their birds, but they're subjecting them to the same factors that exacerbate heart disease in humans—a diet too high in fat and a sedentary lifestyle."

Left in Dr. Varner's care, this parrot was put on a strict diet and a course of antibiotics for several weeks before she judged him well enough to go home. The vet staff left many messages for his owner to come and pick him up, but after a month, there was no response. Dr. Varner realized that no one would be coming to claim Amigo. Once again, he needed a new home.

She had seen this sad scenario play out before, and not just with birds. Owners unable or unwilling to pay an animal's bill will never come back to retrieve it. Some intend to abandon the birds from the start. Ever since the first time I saw Dr. Varner with the dying dove, there had always been a few such "exotics" caged in a back room, awaiting homes. Some of them were in woeful condition, having lost most of their feathers from self-plucking, a result of stress. A nearly naked parrot, with its short legs and large head, looks a bit like E.T. A vet must use all her healing arts and a lot of TLC to bring a bird back to an adoptable state of health. Given Dr. Varner's experience with abandoned patients, the clinic kept a list of people who had inquired about adopting a bird. "Special needs" birds—those with disabilities or behavioral issues—sometimes took a few weeks to place. On the other hand, a healthy bird was often settled into a new home after just a few phone calls.

Amigo was slimmed down and well. He was a bit cranky but manageable. Better still, he was a red-headed Amazon, a species native to northeastern Mexico. Red-headed Amazons had become seriously endangered in the wild owing to illegal trapping and habitat destruction; very few were still available as pets. Dr. Varner had been pretty confident that a bird so robust, handsome, talkative, and rare would be a breeze to place. Potential adopters began arriving immediately. Just as quickly, they headed for the door. One departing prospect suggested a name change. "You ought to call him Rambo."

Who isn't grumpy on a stringent diet and medical treatments? Amigo had become so fed up that he had begun to attack techs who approached just to feed him or clean his cage. He was quick with his beak, and when he struck he managed to draw blood from even the most wary staffers. By the time the adoption visitations began, Amigo would lunge fiercely at any interloper, chest down in attack position, beak wide open. Clearly this often-rehomed little guy had reason to get fearful and feisty at the parade of human gawkers. If anyone came too close to the wire bars on his cage, he would inflict a nasty bite. The warning sign went up when even the most experienced vet techs could not evade the bird's attacks. They drew lots to determine who would clean his cage.

The situation had become untenable for Amigo and for Dr. Varner. She had concluded that he was simply not adoptable in his aggressive state. He would have to stay locked up in a veterinary hospital—frustrated, alone, increasingly fierce, and taking up expensive clinic space and staff time. The sad standoff could have lasted for years, even decades.

Enter Nick, the chosen boy.

I wondered at the randomness of Amigo's sudden courtship. Certainly our growing flock at home made me more attuned to and accepting of the emotional lives of birds. But did anyone expect me to believe that a bird with a brain the size of a hickory nut had planned this clever ambush? Dr. Varner seemed convinced that Amigo had taken the initiative in order to improve his own fate. "He probably decided that this time around he was done with bad placements," she theorized. "It could be he was determined to get a boy, someone young he could train."

This sounded daft at the time. Little did I dream that macaws and African grays would come to train me like savvy ringmasters.

The good doctor also knew my susceptibility to animal hard-luck stories, and she was not above plucking a few heartstrings to make her case.

"Isn't it time that Amigo got a real home with someone he loves?"

Seeing my hesitation, she offered to sweeten the deal. "You don't have to make a commitment right away. Why not a trial run? Would you take Amigo for a few weeks and see how it works out?"

For every objection I voiced—more vet bills, expensive food—she had a counter: Several months of free food, plus free vet care for a year. She'd toss in a carrier and a few toys. Finally I caved. When we walked back into the examining room to tell Nick and his new companion the news, the doctor and I agreed on one ironclad condition for Nick: "We can only take Amigo home—on a trial basis—if you promise that you will never carry him on your shoulder."

This would become an ironclad Pandemonium rule as well. Given parrots' biting issues, carrying such birds at arm's length from vulnerable eyes, noses, and lips is the safest way to go. Dr. Varner taught Nick the proper way to hold the bird on his hand. She demonstrated, putting a hand out for Amigo to step up onto. For the first time in months, he went to her without hesitation. The techs were aghast. Our new carrier had been placed on the table. Nick told Amigo that as soon as he walked into it, we could go home. "You'll live in my room," he promised. Amigo strutted briskly toward his deliverance.

AS AMIGO STEPPED boldly into our lives, the door opened a crack for a growing and raucous convocation of companion-bird rescues. The sanctuary couldn't have grown as it did if I hadn't let emotion trump logic—at least sometimes. I listened to my heart that day, enough to hear the longing in my son's voice. Could I deprive him of a deep and satisfying connection with a needy bird? What could be bad?

By the time the clinic staffers helped us carry the medicated dove, Amigo, and his accoutrements to the car, I was already thinking about the necessary household adjustments. At that point, all of our birds, about seventy-five, were in the outside aviaries. Now we had a "house" parrot.

As it happened, we had conducted a lively family debate on parrot ownership just a couple of weeks earlier, when a breeder had offered me an adorable brother-and-sister pair of baby eclectus parrots. The species is native to Australia, New Guinea, and the Solomon Islands. As rare "sexually dimorphic" parrots, the eclectus babies were very differently colored: males are vivid green, and females are red and blue. They are valued as companion birds for their intelligence and language acquisition. Our whole family had gone to look at the babies. They were so winsome that instead of invoking the customary mantra ("No more birds!"), Tom and the kids all lobbied for me to bring them home.

I did pretty extensive research on parrot care shortly after the breeder had offered me the eclectus babies, and I had turned up many reasons to run the other way. A home needs to be parrot-proofed of more potential hazards than generally beset a human baby. Exotic birds can be undone by Teflon pans, scented candles, air fresheners, ceiling fans, an open window. More fun: random pooping and high-decibel screaming—just fine in a jungle canopy but excruciating in a suburban split ranch. I discovered that I would have to cook special meals for the birds and shower with them (or supervise them on specially installed shower perches) at least every other day to clear their feathers of dust and dander. (They are native to rain forests, remember.) They would require an expensive, commodious new cage, a rotation of stimulating new toys, and daily exercise and socialization time. With three rowdy boys and preteen Lizzy in the house, and our multiplying aviaries, I feared for my stamina and my sanity.

The scariest phrase in the parrot literature—used over and over—was "perpetual toddler." The analogy fits. While there is great variation between and within avian species, experiments have shown that parrots can understand and speak meaningfully in human languages, follow directions, and do math at the level of an average three- or four-year-old child. Their emotional intelligence is also very well developed. Most studies equate it with that of a two- or three-year-old child.

Think about it: a preschooler's lively curiosity plus the mercurial mood swings of the "terrible twos." Over the family's pleading, I delivered a loud and emphatic no. Now here I was with a very feisty, serially rehomed parrot—a known biter—on the backseat beside our son.

For most of the ride home, Nick had been as chatty as I was silent. "You're gonna love my room," he said, directing his voice into the carrier. "I'll fix it up for you." There were more burbles from Amigo. We were nearly home when I realized another issue I'd forgotten to raise at the vet's. We had no cage. Nick leaned over and told Amigo not to sweat it. "You'll live under my bed."

It worked for all of us. For the first time in his young life, Nick kept the floor of his room utterly free of clutter "because Amigo might get lost in it." He mopped up droppings promptly, without complaint. Amigo seemed secure and comfortable housed beneath his beloved. Never an early riser, Nick came to obey his feathered alarm clock. Every morning, Amigo would leave his sleeping spot under the bed, climb up the covers with beak and claws, zero in on Nick's hair, and groom him until he woke up.

Nick would try to put him off. "Go away. Go back to sleep." Amigo was undeterred. If gentle persuasion didn't work, he would launch a thunderous salvo directly into Nick's ear: "Amigo! Amigo! Amigo!" The screeches were always the charm: Nick heaved himself up and rushed to the kitchen to prepare Amigo's breakfast of pellets and fresh fruit. Like so many middle school boys, Nick would have been happy to forgo bathing for days on end. His bird needed to be bathed, though, so he took lengthy showers. Daily. Dr. Varner had not included a special shower perch in our farewell kit, but I found one at a local pet shop.

Whatever they were doing, boy and bird communicated incessantly. At least that's what Nick said. I couldn't understand Amigo's gravelly natter, so I assumed that Nick was adding his own coloration when he'd say things like, "Amigo was telling me about his day," or "Amigo was telling me about his life before he found me."

When Nick was off at school, Amigo spent a good part of the day beneath the bed, playing with his toys or dozing. Parrots do need plenty of sleep. Once he had settled into the household routine, Amigo began amusing himself with a curious Socratic monologue.

"Why? Why not?"

Hearing that small voice inquiring from beneath the bed was pretty cute the first few times the family heard it. We called him our philosopher-parrot. But after a few hundred times, we were muttering about a cup of hemlock. Even Nick had had enough of the tedious recitation.

One day, after Amigo's first, "Why?" Nick interjected, "Why not?"

There was silence for a few seconds. Then quietly, from beneath the bed: "I don't know."

It was over, just like that.

Nick always followed Dr. Varner's rule prohibiting shoulder carrying. But an active boy found hand-carrying his pal cumbersome. They came up with a solution that worked for both of them. Amigo clamped his beak to the bottom of Nick's shirt. This let him stay connected regardless of what Nick was doing. If his boy ran, Amigo hung tough, his little body swinging back and forth.

It wasn't long before all Nick's shirts were shot with multiple holes. Some were so ratty that I told him they could no longer be worn to school. "But Mom," Nick countered, "everyone wears their shirts like this now." And they did. A bit of checking around revealed that Nick and Amigo had started a middle school fad. The other students were imitating Nick's punky, parrot-distressed look by using sharpened pencils or scissors to trash their shirts. Luckily none of the other moms figured out who was responsible for starting this fashion-forward deconstruction.

"I love you, I love you!" Amigo declared to Nick constantly. Tom was not so fortunate. He had always been kind and attentive to our son's new companion, yet whenever Tom walked into the room, Amigo would glare at him and mutter, "Asshole!" Maybe Tom reminded the bird of a mean former owner. We'll never know. The expletive delighted Nick and his pals, who howled with glee every time the bird let loose with it. Amigo was only encouraged by their response. No matter the distance, even if Tom was way out in the backyard, the little foulmouth would holler, "Asshole!" at top volume. Mercifully our neighbors are a good distance away.

Amigo had no pet name for me, but I was singled out for more special treatment. He bit me—often, and with such stealth and cunning I had to half admire his success. One possible reason for his disdain: Parrots have long memories. During the debates with Dr. Varner about adoption, Amigo may have noticed my tone of voice, my body language, and my negative "bad cop" vibe. It's likely he had some prior associations with a loud, "Uh-uh, no way!"

It didn't matter that I soon recognized the lowered chest, the sidelong glare. Once it was clear I had learned those danger signals, Amigo changed tactics. He'd go sweet on me, crouching and fluttering his wings, a sign that he wanted to be picked up. I'd melt. He seemed to like traveling around the house on my hand. Amigo couldn't fly. We had complied with Dr. Varner's strong advice to clip his wings so that he could not fly off, especially since I would be moving him between indoor and outdoor perches. Flightlessness seemed a reasonable compromise for a warm and loving home, but I did feel bad about it.

Amigo was acting almost conciliatory. He would execute his flutter routine, I'd extend my hand, and he'd step up like a gentleman. We were finally becoming friends. Once I was lulled into goofy complacency, he started asking to be picked up and then biting—hard—at my extended hand. If I hollered,

"Ouch!" he would burst into laughter. "Ha-ha-ha!" The boys, hearing him laugh, always joined in. That only egged him on. I developed a fine network of fading scars. But despite our jousting, I grew fond of our devilish new family member. Maybe it was like learning to love a difficult daughter-in-law: you make allowances when someone loves your son, madly and truly.

Nick was surely a better young man for their partnership. He was devoted, constant, responsible, and ever vigilant of his tiny buddy. When that moment all parents dread arrived and Nick got his driver's license, he didn't head out to pick up his friends. He asked politely to use the car, gathered two towels, and, with Amigo in tow, took off for the park where I used to take Nick when he was small. They went often. One day, I asked to join them.

Amigo rode in the backseat with one of the towels spread on it. The second towel was laid out to reserve a spot on the park lawn while Nick took Amigo with him on the swings and the slide. The flightless parrot loved those joyrides. Mothers, children, dog walkers, and Frisbee players all seemed to know Amigo and called out to him by name. Should a dog come too near, Nick would scoop up his bird. He explained patiently to children that they couldn't "pet" his parrot. This tender care was not typical of the teenager I knew at home. That one had become a surly door slammer who was most uncommunicative with his human family. I knew it would pass, as it had with his older brothers. I was grateful for the civility that Amigo still commanded.

Still, I wondered. Nick would most likely be leaving for college soon. What then? Would Amigo tolerate us? Pine for his best pal? We had some time to think about it. I was sure of one thing, though. Whatever it took, this remarkable little bird would never need rehoming again.

# SEVEN

# Wing and Coffee:
# Crowned Glories

"Michele, I've got an offer you can't refuse."

Aviculturists who breed for profit can't afford to be too sentimental, so when Louis Brown called to offer me a female Victoria crowned pigeon—almost for free—I assumed that he had no use for her, even though he loves the species. At the time, these oversize blue pigeons from New Guinea were selling for about $1,500, if they were healthy and able to breed. But Louis admitted that this one was damaged merchandise.

She had a broken wing. He felt it wasn't economically viable to have it repaired. Handicapped birds are usually a liability to a breeder because they are more difficult to mate. Worse, Victoria crowneds are fairly pricey to keep. They require a lot of space and a specialized diet of fruit, vegetables, seed, and a protein source to replace the fallen fruit and invertebrates that they gather from the forest floors of New Guinea. I would also find out later that they don't tolerate cold weather well. If they are not given supplemental heat in Northern California winters, there can be expensive vet bills to pay.

Michele will take her! That was fast becoming the off-loading strategy of the breeding community. Some breeders regularly killed birds that were no longer paying their way. Very few of them liked doing this, but they felt they had no other option. So when word got around that a lady was willing to take unwanted birds as long as you told her a sob story about what would happen if she *didn't* take them—and that she was also crazy enough to find and buy mates for lonely adopted birds—well, start punching her number into your phone before that lorikeet breeder beats you to it. Some days these "gift" offers were so numerous and insistent, I couldn't even listen to my messages.

Of course I said yes to Louis's crippled Victoria crowned. I made arrangements to drive up and get the bird the following day. When Louis brought her out, I felt concern rather than excitement. She was beautiful, with her vivid, red-rimmed eyes and rippling crown of white-tipped feathers. The bird had been dropped from a feeding table when she was three weeks old, and the injured wing had never healed properly. As a full-grown adult, she looked as if she was tilting to one side because she dragged the damaged wing on the floor. Maybe that's why she was named Wing.

She was a sorry sight, and so withdrawn and affectless I didn't warm to her. Wing did not care for the company of humans, nor did she enjoy being petted like most of her docile, sociable species. Once I brought her home, I discussed her depressed state with a new vet who had come by for a visit. Anne Calloway was a young doctor who had just joined a dog and cat practice and had a long-standing love of birds. Since veterinary care is often assigned by voucher from shelters and rescue groups, our birds have been cared for by a number of different, excellent practitioners.

Anne was on her way to becoming a certified avian specialist. Meeting her had been another bit of random luck. Like Dr. Varner, Anne would become a dear friend and gentle healer to many Pandemonium birds. "Wing has the personality of a pheasant—aloof and wary," I told her. "I suppose she's afraid of being hurt again."

Anne disagreed. "I don't think her personality has a psychological basis. I think that Wing's behavior might be due to her being in physical pain. Mind if I take her in and do an X-ray?"

The results were disturbing. The broken wing looked like swiss cheese inside. "The tissue is a mess," Anne said. "If you want to prevent further damage, we need to take off all or at least part of the wing." I felt bad that I hadn't taken Wing in for an exam sooner. Who knew how long she'd been in pain? I agreed to the surgery on the wing. We decided to do an amputation with the minimum possible tissue removed, but this turned out to be a mistake. Wing had to have a second operation several months later to remove what remained of her wing.

Once she had healed and was no longer in pain, she became much more social, just as Anne had predicted.

Still, the bird needed something more than good medicine, and in my heart I knew exactly what it should be. When Louis called again and offered me Wing's brother Coffee at a steep discount, I jumped at the chance to get her a close companion. Unlike his sister, Coffee was Mr. Personality around the Browns' rambling spread. In fact, he was almost a lap bird, too tame to breed and therefore of no use to Louis in expanding his flock. I brought Coffee home and opened his carrier in the living room. When he stepped out into his new life, he had a proprietary air about him. Soon I found out why: Coffee considered himself a house pet, with full family privileges.

Calmly the bird inspected the living room as I watched, seated on the floor. As he walked, he wagged his tail from side to side like a happy puppy, and then he stopped and called out with a loud "*boom, boooom.*" Louis had told me the bird was named Coffee because he liked to sit on Louis's lap and sip out of his coffee mug. I was puzzled, since I'd just been reading about foods poisonous to birds, and coffee was listed as dangerous to the point of causing cardiac arrest. Louis must have been having a little fun with me; as I'd find out, sometimes his tales were as colorful as his birds. Coffee kept his name, though.

When he was finished exploring the living room, Coffee walked up and nibbled at my big toe. Realizing that the toe was not edible, he looked up at me and opened and closed his beak several times. I recognized that as bird talk for hunger. I raced to the kitchen for some grapes and put them on the floor. He eyed them, looked at me, and did the beak thing again. Was this big baby used to being hand-fed?

I picked up a grape and put it on my open palm in front of his beak. He pecked at my hand a few times but didn't connect with the grape. After each attempt he'd look up and stare, all the while opening and closing his beak. Something about this bird's gaze, the soft but insistent way he continued to look at me, was captivating. I picked up the grape with my left hand, held his beak open with my right, and shoved in the grape. Coffee swallowed the grape, made a satisfied purring sound, and did his beak flap again: Please, may I have some more? I stayed there feeding him, staring at the amazing white-tipped crown of feathers that vibrated when he swallowed. I was smitten. Unlike his big sister, this guy had me at "boom."

Left to his own devices, Coffee would have slept in the house like the dogs and cat and spent his days in the fenced yard outside. But for his own safety—and given the remarkable stench of exotic pigeon poop—Coffee would have to live in an aviary. He did not agree; he hung out at the gate disconsolately, waiting for me to bring him his breakfast and scratch his neck. Once I stopped the scratching, he'd look at me sadly and then try to snuggle under my arm. The depression was understandable for a bird that lives in flocks of up to twenty in the wild. Since, like all new residents, Coffee was still under quarantine until I was sure he was healthy, I had to keep him in an aviary alone for a while. But I had plans. Once again, I cajoled Tom.

"Do you mind if I build an enclosure that abuts the house?"

"You're actually asking?" he answered.

At least he was smiling. I had the enclosure built near the side door so that Coffee could see us coming and going. I'd left part of his pen unroofed so that he could enjoy direct sunlight. This was terrific when the sun was shining. But one night, during a fierce rainstorm, I ran outside barefoot to check on Coffee. He was sitting in front of the gate, huddled in a soaking heap. He didn't even look at me when I picked him up, put him inside my raincoat, and brought him inside.

I dried him off as best I could with a kitchen towel and put him on the floor of the laundry room with a bowl of drinking water and went back to bed. The next morning I found that Coffee had made himself comfortable on top of a pile of formerly clean clothes stacked on the dryer. I walked over and scratched his head. He made that odd purring sound. Finally he was where he belonged, inside the house. A case of sniffles kept him there for a while.

In a way, the Victoria crowned's "gregarious nature," as the scant field literature describes it, has helped seal its fate in the wild. At one time the birds were safe in New Guinea forests too dense to penetrate, but now that palm oil companies are forging roads through the forests, the birds are becoming more and more accessible to hunters. The Victoria crowned pigeons' heavy bodies make them awkward and slow fliers. Add to that their innate friendliness—they seem to have little fear of humans, even in the wild—and the species is no match for a hunter.

Though the birds are officially protected in New Guinea, poaching is still a huge problem and there is little or no enforcement of the hunting prohibition. Their splendid feathers are used in headdresses, their skins are sold to tourists, and their meat is consumed. Because they tame easily and quickly, hunters also collect live young Victoria crowneds to keep in pens in much the way Americans keep backyard chickens. They raise them as food, but the birds are not valued as egg producers, since they lay only a single egg at a time and generally no more than three a year. If they are allowed to hatch an egg, both parents incubate it for a month and then nurture the chick for three to five more months. At first the parents feed the babies crop milk, a protein- and fat-rich secretion of the crop, a pouch near the bird's throat that is part of its digestive system. Both male and female Victoria crowneds produce crop milk. The only other birds able to produce this nourishment besides pigeon species are flamingos.

This is excellent nutrition for wild babies but problematic should a breeder have to hand-raise a Victoria crowned chick with some alternative nutrient source. But I'm getting ahead of myself. When we welcomed our first Victoria crowneds, Coffee and Wing, I was sure I would *never* be breeding them, even by accident. Because they were siblings, I made sure that they had no nesting box or materials to support breeding. If they did manage to produce an egg, I intended to remove it.

The moment I was able to reunite Wing and Coffee in the Blue Butterfly Aviary, a bright, airy space big enough for both of them, they stared at each other and broke into a run. They began grooming each other immediately, pulling solicitously at neck feathers in an avian form of embrace. Cue the violins: I sat there sniffling at the sight of such pure joy.

How Louis would have laughed at the messy sight of me there. I was surely savoring the moment, but the big picture for this breed is not so rosy. Continued reports are still so dire about Victoria crowneds in the wild that it seems their best chance of survival on their native island is on an official Papua New Guinea postage stamp, finely etched, gummed, and perforated. I have some; they're gorgeous.

But why settle for such a sad, one-inch-square epitaph if the birds could still boom across the earth . . . *somewhere*?

# EIGHT

# Let's Have Babies

I'll be honest, I don't connect instantly with all birds that come into our sanctuary. I was a diligent caregiver to the mated pair of green-naped pheasant pigeons (hereafter shortened as GNPPs) that had arrived unbidden in the mail that day from my "bird friend" Larry, who had split with his partner. Once I saw them in the sunlight, I realized that these somewhat ungainly-looking birds did have a unique sort of beauty. Their backs turn iridescent teal in the sun, and their commitment to each other was impressive. They always moved in tandem, bodies nearly touching; it was rare to find them more than a few feet apart. They were interested only in each other and ran from any human entering their aviary. I hadn't even been engaged enough to name them until a trip to the vet required names for the registration forms.

At the clinic's intake desk, I quickly pronounced the couple Guinevere (Gwen) and Lancelot. Their romantic attachment was something out of Camelot—so much so that I brought them both to the clinic, though only Gwen was ill, with a throat abscess. The pair had never been separated, and I felt the stress of being apart would be harmful to both—especially to the ailing Gwen. It turned out that she needed surgery on her throat, which was performed.

The stay at the veterinary clinic was upsetting to both of them; when I went to retrieve them, their backs were both featherless from being handled. Many dove species lose their feathers when they are handled or frightened; shedding feathers instantly is both a panic response and a gambit for escaping the grip of predators in the wild. Hawks and coyotes are often left with talons or mouths full of feathers as their prey soars away. When I got them home, I worried that the chill weather might be fatal to a postsurgical bird from a tropical climate—especially now that Gwen had large areas of exposed skin. In they both came; I made them warm and comfortable in a plastic-draped spare bedroom. They stayed in the house for two and a half months. By the time they had regrown their feathers, the weather had warmed up and we had become friends. Almost.

I moved them into the easily monitored Blue Butterfly Aviary. They no longer ran away when I entered their space. If I came in carrying some juicy mealworms, they would approach to within an arm's distance. It wasn't the first time that once-standoffish birds had changed their attitude toward me after being ill or stressed and closely cared for. My own feelings had changed as well. I took a real liking to this devoted pigeon pair. I looked forward to seeing them on my morning rounds. I talked, they tolerated me.

And then, a random accident. I was sitting at the kitchen table with the newspaper one Saturday morning when I heard *Pop! Crack!* It sounded like pistol shots. I ran outside and found no crazed intruder or smoking gun—just a torrent of water gushing from broken faucets throughout the yard. The city had recently installed an underground water-pressure regulator that turned out to be defective. The built-up pressure blew the lines on our property. Aviaries that had faucets in them had large and growing puddles, yet the birds—the ones I could see— seemed fine.

But I was concerned about another exotic trait of the green-napeds. They have an extreme startle reflex, and though they are pigeons, green-napeds flush straight up, like pheasants. Nest boxes must have soft tops lest the birds hit their heads or break their necks. An unexpected loud noise can be as lethal as a bullet.

I found Gwen dead on her nest, which did have the pre-cautionary soft top. She had been incubating an egg. The pair had tried to nest many times, without success. I felt that I should act fast and raced to the house for a plastic bag. I put the body in the bag, together with the egg, picked up the nest box, and took them away. As I made my way out of the avi-ary, a crepe myrtle blossom fell on my head from the tree that shaded the aviary. I didn't notice it until I looked in a mirror much later. I wish now that I'd pressed it between the pages of a book, as a reminder of those unpredictable early days. Every time I thought I had figured something out—like getting these birds healthy and acclimated—I was soon proved wrong.

I took Gwen's corpse to the vet for a necropsy; we do post-mortems on all birds that die, the better to understand their deaths and care for the rest of the birds. I shouldn't have taken away the dead bird so quickly, but I didn't know better. I didn't think about the mate she was leaving behind. If he didn't see her die or find her body or the egg or the nest box, how would he know what had happened to her? His reaction would be one of puzzlement and panic: Where did my mate go? When will she be back?

For the first couple of days after Gwen was gone, Lancelot kept a vigil huddled in the corner of the aviary where the nest had been. He barely moved. Meanwhile the necropsy report came back. There were indications of a fatal heart attack: Gwen had been startled to death. After a few days had passed, Lancelot moved outside under the crepe myrtle tree. Early one morning, I was jolted awake by a raw, heartrending cry. It kept up, growing louder and louder. I followed the sound to the Blue Butterfly Aviary. Lancelot stood with his head thrown back as if to vocalize a terrible grief.

The cries rose, ragged and sharp over the general avian din, and on it went, day and night. I needed to find another GNPP hen, as soon as possible. I thought about those first doves of

Eileen's that may well have perished from their separation. Lancelot wasn't eating well and I was worried. It occurred to me that his call was only partially a widower's lament; it was also a vocal advertisement for a new mate. I resolved to track one down for Lancelot.

I had no idea how involved such a search would be. Nobody had GNPPs—or at least no breeder would admit to it. After hundreds of phone calls and countless hours of research, I learned that there were only thirty-two green-napeds in all the world's zoos and probably fewer than a hundred in captivity in private collections. Louis Brown told me that his pairs had died, but he made calls for me to zoos and other breeders. He tried all his closely guarded connections, with no luck. Even if someone did have green-napeds, it was unlikely that they would sell such a rare hen to a novice breeder like me. I was known only for taking unwanted birds. Outside, Lancelot cried and wailed.

Finally I was able to buy a GNPP hen from a breeder roundly disliked for his unscrupulous dealings. Doing business with him was a last resort, and he probably gouged us on the price, but it was worth it. Lancelot settled down nicely with his new lady, and I sat down for a hard look at our inventory.

I had been shocked to learn how rare the GNPPs had become, and now I wanted to know whether we had any other birds in imminent danger of disappearing. A friend who had access to the bird census figures on the International Species Information System (ISIS) gave us data on the location, number, and sex of birds in two hundred facilities worldwide.

I discovered that fourteen species living in our aviaries had become rare and were highly coveted by breeders and zoos. According to the census, few of these birds were in mated pairs. So I set about gifting some of the individual birds to capable people with the interest and ability to breed them. I gave away four species of doves—golden heart, crested quail-doves, blue ground, and Key West quail-doves. But I couldn't bear to part with two species: the Victoria crowned pigeons and the GNPPs. They were so unique in the world.

Yet I felt that keeping them bestowed a certain responsibility. I should breed them to help keep their species viable. For years I had ignored the breeding side of my work—discouraging certain birds from breeding, even as I sought out mates for them—because I wanted to maximize space for rescues. I now had to play catch-up. Learning conservation breeding would be daunting. I'd essentially backed into everything else about Pandemonium; at least I was going into this new phase of the organization with my eyes wide open. Sort of. Beginning with my resolve to breed the GNPPs, our sanctuary would gradually change from an opportunistic mode—taking in diverse species of rescue birds as the need arose—to a more strategic operation. The old softy in me had always bought birds as companions for some of the lonely and alienated rescue birds. Michele the budding conservationist would have to become a focused aviculturist always on the lookout for healthy breeding stock.

It was a different, more severe form of bird fever. The mission became conservation, the compulsion more urgent. Both Browns had cautioned me about getting in too deep. Carol told me stories of bird keepers whose health had been seriously affected by the demands of a job that had no days off. They both suggested that I specialize—select a species or two that I really liked and stick to those. I remember thinking, But I do specialize. I specialize in everything.

My search for Lancelot's new mate had pushed me deeper into a pretty exclusive brotherhood, since female breeders are as rare as some of the birds. My inquiries were often met with wariness or dismissal. Breeders and collectors are secretive about what they have; they often react with suspicion to strangers and novices. One key to gaining acceptance is to have successfully bred a species that is difficult and rare. Since even Louis had had no success with the GNPPs, I was probably setting myself up for failure. The only way to improve my odds was to build up my knowledge.

I'd have to find out what my GNPPs required for nesting, and how to tell they were "sitting" without disturbing that very crucial process. It's always best that birds incubate their own eggs and feed their hatchlings, but sometimes they are unable to do so in captivity or will abandon eggs. We never take eggs from nesting birds unless it's absolutely necessary for their survival. Then it's up to us to see whether we can supervise a successful hatch.

The Browns would be a superb resource when it came to the science—incubating eggs, hatching them, and caring for the babies. No one is better with eggs than Carol. When I visited, she was often on the phone calming nervous egg watchers from Florida to San Diego. The other component of breeding—the "art" of acquiring and pairing up breeding stock, which is Louis's specialty—is an intuitive gift not easily passed on.

It made sense, then, to start with the science. I needed some basic tutorials on the process of incubation. I pored over aviculture journals and websites and, to my great excitement, found a hands-on course I could not afford to miss. SeaWorld in San Diego was offering a zookeeper's course in egg incubation, taught by Susie Kasielke, well known in aviculture for her work on the conservation breeding of the giant California condors.

I realized during the first few hours of those classes that despite the difficulties, this new challenge was utterly fascinating. We worked with fertilized chicken eggs at various stages of development. Even though I had kept backyard chickens, I was amazed by the biological process that brings a chick of any sort out of its protective shell and into the wide, perilous world. The eggs that we worked with were "smoked"—rendered nonviable at various stages of development. We opened them and did egg necropsies to see and identify the progressive stages.

We first learned how to weigh the egg and measure the water lost through respiration as gestation progressed, how to "candle" an egg to assess the developing chick and locate its essential air cell within the egg, and how to tell if the baby is positioned correctly with the head under the left wing, near the air cell. We practiced how and when to turn an incubating egg as the parents would, how to use a heart monitor and recognize signs of an imminent hatching. We learned how to do an "assisted hatch" to help the baby come out if it was in trouble. What I had always viewed as commonplace seemed utterly miraculous. I headed home eager to get started, but I knew I wasn't ready yet to tackle breeding the GNPPs.

Instead I began with plum-headed parakeets, for two reasons. First, I knew that the species was desirable and hard to come by. These stunning little birds from India have bright green bodies and distinctive purple heads. They had been very popular as pets because of their compact size, beauty, and gentle, endearing personalities. But their popularity had fallen off once the Wild Bird Act made it all but impossible to import more breeding stock. If I were successful in producing offspring, I could use them as "chits" in exchange for other birds that I needed. (At the top of my wish list was, of course, a GNPP hen.) The other compelling reason to try plum-heads was that they aren't endangered, so if I made mistakes, I wouldn't contribute to wiping out a species.

Our first plum-head had come from a humane society. Then

a pair sent to us from another rescue group in Denver endured an incredible journey when a shipping error sent them to San José, Costa Rica, instead of San Jose, California. When they finally arrived, we named the weary travelers Costa and Rica. Boy, did we have babies. Adorable little purple heads bobbed in plenty of nesting boxes. I learned a good deal about breeding, made some excellent swaps, and kept a weather eye out for that elusive GNPP hen. I was pretty proud of my trajectory toward a more empirical, hard-nosed sort of aviculture—until I tripped over a heartstring. Again.

Sweetie had been at Pandemonium for several years, enjoying the company of several other coturnix quail I had added. I noticed that he was limping. When I picked him up, I saw a cut at the bottom of his foot. It wasn't particularly deep, but it had gone unnoticed long enough to become infected. After Dr. Varner examined Sweetie, he was not hopeful. "These birds don't do especially well on antibiotics. You can try, but I don't think it will help. He'll have to be on them for a long time."

The course of treatment amounted to weeks of torture for Sweetie; he was confined to a small hospital cage and had to endure force-fed medicine twice a day. Soon even the extra worms I gave him did not lift his mood. The infection would seem to clear, only to flare up again once we stopped treatment.

Dr. Varner finally suggested that euthanasia was the kindest option; instead I took Sweetie to another avian specialist two hours away. The second vet's alternative course of antibiotics and a subsequent surgery only made the quail more miserable. I'd convince myself that I should arrange for euthanasia, but every time I thought about life without Sweetie, I couldn't take the step of hastening his death.

When finally he rallied a bit after the surgery, I was about to take him home from the second vet's. He ate a mealworm that was in his carrier. It was a good sign. He picked up the second worm, but never got a chance to swallow it. He seized up and died quickly, without pain and right in the middle of his favorite activity.

When I had stopped crying long enough to speak, I ask the vet a question. "What is the life span of a cortunix quail?"

"Don't know," he answered. "They're usually slaughtered when they're young, so I have no idea how long they could live, but I'd be surprised if it is more than a couple of years. Your quail was a real old-timer if you had him more than that."

He turned to leave but came back. "Sweetie was the first quail I have ever treated," he told me. "We don't usually get game birds brought in here. I'll tell you one thing: that little bird of yours had such a dynamite and friendly personality, it's wrecked my appetite for birds like this. I won't be eating quail again."

I tried to smile. When I got home, I turned to a quotation that was never far from my desk, from a book called *Separate Lifetimes* by Irving Townsend. Townsend was a renowned record producer for the likes of Miles Davis. He was also an author who wrote about the intimate connections between humans and their pets. The passage that has solaced so many grieving pet owners helped once again as I said good-bye to the tiny bird who taught me so much: "We who choose to surround ourselves with lives even more temporary than our own, live within a fragile circle, easily and often breached. Unable to accept its awful gaps, we still would live no other way. We cherish memory as the only certain immortality, never fully understanding the necessary plan."

# NINE

# Mail-Order Bride

On those TV reality shows about animal rescue, the abuses are often appallingly clear—emaciated dogs and cats, skeletal horses, all delivered from their suffering by uniformed officers in shiny vans. Bird rescues are quite different.

Imagine a call coming in: "Dispatch, we have a lorikeet being fed birdseed!"

"Copy that, we'll get an investigator over there ASAP!"

What average person would see cruelty—possibly fatal—looking at a pretty parrot with a dish full of seed? The clues to abuse, neglect, and illness in birds are often not apparent to the untrained eye. As we found with Amigo, a robust, good-looking parrot can actually be in serious danger from obesity. As a rescuer, you really have to know what to look for.

One day I received a call from a local bird rescue group to stand by for a possible adoption. They had received a phone tip about a rainbow lorikeet seen at the Bird Mart, an avian bazaar held every three months or so in our area in a large hall at the fairgrounds. Bird and bird supply vendors come from miles away to sell their goods at prices that are considerably below those at pet stores. The people selling birds are either small backyard breeders or brokers. Most accept cash only—and good luck finding them afterward if you have questions or problems with your purchase. The birds sold are sometimes sick and are sent to their new homes with few or no care instructions.

The rescue informant clearly knew about rainbow lorikeets. They are medium-size parrots, about ten inches high, native to Australia and a few smaller Pacific islands. Their colors are stunning: royal-blue heads with bright red beaks, green bodies, and a ruffled bib of scarlet across their chests. Lorikeets are now protected in Australia, where they have long been marketable as pets. They're pretty, congenial, and cheerfully antic. They subsist on fruit, pollen, and nectar, and their tongues have a sticky appendage at the end to gather their food from deep within blossoms. They are not meant to eat seed, except as part of the fresh fruits they consume. Giving them a dried seed diet can result in sick, malnourished birds.

The rescue group told me that they were sending a volunteer to the Bird Mart to have a look. If she felt the bird was in serious trouble, she was to buy it and bring it to me. They would put up the purchase funds if I agreed to keep the parrot. At the market, the volunteer found only one vendor selling lorikeets; he had two of them, from different lorikeet subspecies. The rescuer approached the vendor and pointed out that the lorikeets' food dishes were full of seed and had gone untouched. The vendor brushed her off. "Don't worry about them. They'll be fine. They're just not hungry—too much excitement here."

She was not reassured. If the vendor didn't know how to feed these lorikeets, he was unlikely to give the right feeding advice to any buyer, and the birds would die. One of the birds didn't look too bad, but the other was in awful shape. His feathers were dull and he lacked the vitality and energy that is characteristic of lorikeets. It was certainly possible that the wrong diet had in effect put him on death row.

The volunteer had been given only enough money to buy one bird, so she pointed to the sick-looking bird and told the seller, "I'll take that one." As she was walking away with the lorikeet we later named Peeki, both birds continued to call to each other frantically. The bird left behind clung screeching to the wire side of its cage. Peeki pressed his head as close as possible to a hole in the carrier so that he could look at his former cage mate as he was being carried away.

The two were clearly more than passing acquaintances. Their behavior suggested they were a bonded pair that the seller had split up, either ignorant of the trauma for the birds or insensitive to it. In the wild, lorikeets live and travel in bonded pairs. The woman had walked the length of the hall with the rescued bird when the caged lorikeet managed to escape. It flew to Peeki's carrier and landed on top of it. The two birds began a frenzied vocalizing back and forth. The seller did not have any trouble retrieving the escaped bird because it remained clinging to Peeki's carrier instead of flying away at his approach.

"How much is this other lorikeet?" the rescuer asked. She felt terrible about separating the pair. "Already sold, but these guys aren't." The vendor pointed to a cage full of doves with dirty tail feathers. When trying to buy the second lorikeet proved fruitless, she left with Peeki and brought him to me. When I heard her story about the sad separation, I was determined to restore his health, then find him a companion. I never imagined that he'd end up with a mail-order bride from the East Coast who spoke like a cast member from *Jersey Shore*.

Once Peeki was recovered and on a proper diet of fruits and nectar, I put out feelers for a female Lorikeet. A New York rescue operation offered me Harli, who was said to be lively, talkative, and friendly. No one quite understood why she had been returned quickly by a string of adopters. I paid for her airfare, and Harli was shipped to California. When she arrived, I brought the travel crate into the house. I opened the carrier door, but it was faulty and fell off. Harli flew out of the crate, directly at Tom. She landed on his shoulder and promptly stuck her long, nectar-probing tongue in his ear.

"Michele, please get her off me!" he said, trying not to yell. "I've been violated by a bird!"

As I reached for her, Harli yawped in a Jersey girl accent, "Whatcha doin', honey?"

Tom and I were helpless with laughter.

Since Harli was not acclimated to the outdoors and she needed to be in quarantine before I introduced her to Peeki, I kept her in my office for a while. I enjoyed her company. Our best times were in the early morning, when I do paperwork. Harli would con me into taking her out of her cage, wriggle out of my hands, settle on my head, and inspect my hair for bugs. I assured her that my head was parasite-free, but she decided it was her job to ensure it remained that way. She also liked to kindly pluck a hair or two while she was searching for imaginary arthropods. By the time her quarantine period was over, I had a small, perfectly shaped oval of bare scalp on the top of my head. Harli could sense when I was about to stop working. I'd be putting the finishing touches on an e-mail, and she'd gather up the hairs that she had harvested, fly over to the chair where our cat, Minx, was curled up asleep, and drop the bundle on Minx's head. Minx would wake up, startled and confused. By the time she noticed the ready-made hair ball, Harli would be across the room, looking utterly innocent.

Harli's exuberance was undiminished when I moved her to an empty outside aviary. "Free food! Free food!" she'd yell happily as I approached to fill her nectar bowl each morning. And to anyone she didn't care for, she bellowed, "Jerk!" But soon another side to this cheery bird emerged. The first time I tried to catch her to have her examined by a vet, I used a towel rather than a net to get ahold of her. She dug her claws into my hand. I had deep puncture wounds that didn't heal for weeks.

Then she started to attack me. Lorikeets have very sharp beaks and nails and can inflict serious damage. Tame lorikeets like Harli can be especially dangerous, since they are not afraid of humans. When Harli flew in your direction, it was impossible to tell whether her intention was to land on your head to groom you or to bite you on the face. I called the rescue group that placed her with me, and they confirmed what I suspected.

Harli had been the adored pet of someone who was unable to cope with behavioral changes when the lorikeet reached puberty. Like humans, animals go through hormonal changes when they reach reproductive age. Most human parents might confess to having inhumane thoughts when their fifteen-year-old morphs into a surly young alien in constant attack mode. ("Eeeew, Mom—are you really going to wear that?") We endure because we know it will pass. In the case of a tame bird, a sudden "attitude" or aggression from a formerly docile creature can be very upsetting to the owner. Unfortunately this sometimes leads to an animal's being given away, even though it is acting naturally. It may begin a self-perpetuating cycle of rejection and aggression.

It's no fun being attacked by a bird, even a little one like Harli. The only way I could get her aviary cleaned was to double-team her. One person did the cleaning while the second stood guard with a net or hose to chase the little dive-bomber away. I took to wearing swim goggles to protect my eyes, and Harli didn't figure out that it was me for some time. Eventually, though, she looked closely at my face and uttered a relieved, "Whatcha doin', honey?"

I didn't think about how odd I must have looked until a new neighbor showed up at the door with a small thank-you gift for a welcoming dinner I had hosted for her family. She thrust a small package at me and said in a cool, dismissive tone, "Give this to the lady of the house. It's very breakable, so be careful." I took the gift and answered politely, as one's household help should, "Certainly, ma'am."

Harli, watching from her aviary, sent the gift giver off with a high-decibel farewell: "Jerk!"

Finally, Harli's quarantine was over and it was time to acquaint her with Peeki. Bird introductions can be tricky. Some birds don't like each other when they first meet, but they grow into the relationship. Others never bond. It's always best to take things slowly. I put Harli's cage next to Peeki's. Both birds stayed as close to each other as they could manage through the wire mesh. I had planned to keep them this way for several days, but after the first day I knew there was no need. I moved their cages into a ten-by-eight-foot aviary and opened both doors at once. The birds flew out of their cages and landed on the same perch, side by side. Harli started preening Peeki, and when she was finished, Peeki did the same for her.

For several years they were a tight, devoted couple; they took baths together, danced or hopped around together, and swung on ropes in tandem. Before Harli's arrival, Peeki had been shy and sedate and never spoke. He was afraid of people and flew to the farthest corner when someone approached him. Once Harli joined him, he became playful. If Harli began her favorite game of swinging upside down from hanging rope pulls, Peeki would be alongside on another rope, keeping pace. He was a strong and agile flier. I suspected from his behavior that he was wild caught and might have spent his carefree Aussie youth in a grove of eucalyptus trees. This made me even more determined to give him the very best quality of life I could; Harli, his ditzy mail-order bride, was one terrific therapist.

We made a convivial trio. Both birds liked to hang upside down on the wire when I approached their aviary. I petted their toenails and talked to them.

"Hi, Harli. Hi, Peeki."

"Harli, Harli, Harli!" Harli would holler back. Peeki stayed right by her side but never said a word. I had put them in the aviary I had built for Coffee and Wing, and since the crowned pigeons were now living in the Blue Butterfly Aviary, I named this one the Lorikeet Lair. It was attached to the house, with a window that opened in. Harli, who had been a family pet, could now have a sense of participating again in human family life. Yet there was space for Peeki to retreat when he wished. He was still his most exuberant self when the two birds were alone. I must have left their feeding door ajar one day, and when I walked into the kitchen sometime later, I found the two lorikeets dancing conga-style around the perimeter of the kitchen table. Harli broke stride just for a second to address the interloper. "Whatcha doin', honey?"

Three was indeed a crowd, so I left them to it.

SPEAKING BIRD—THAT IS, communicating with our Pandemonium flock—had become a great joy, and I was becoming better at it. But I also longed to talk birds with breeders, vets, academics, and other avian obsessives, people who wouldn't roll their eyes when I extemporized over molting patterns and nest box hygiene. I had passed up a number of professional conferences because it was hard to leave the birds. It was a lot of work for a "sitter" to take on, and I worried. Still do.

There was a conference coming up that included a special panel on lorikeet nutrition. The pollen that they would take directly from flowers in the wild is not reproducible, so instead we feed a powder, which the birds themselves mix with water to produce a nectar. It can be a tricky business.

I made arrangements for interim help with the birds, took a deep breath, and packed for the three-day conference. On my way out, I stopped to say good-bye to the lorikeets. Harli was hanging upside down on her favorite rope swing next to Peeki. "See you when I come back," I sang out. Harli answered, "See ya later, honey!" as she vigorously pumped the swing.

The aviculture conference was better than I'd imagined. I learned a lot, loved the company of like-minded bird keepers, and was thrilled to be able to exchange information for hours at a time. I arrived home feeling energized. The rest of the family was off visiting relatives, so I went to check on the birds and say hello to the dogs and cat. As I walked down the stone path to my front door, there was a chorus of "Hello," "Hi," and "How *are* you?" from the parrots and a cacophony of honks and whistles from the Australian parakeets. But the Lorikeet Lair was silent. Harli always greeted me by yelling out an energetic, "Harli! Harli!" whenever she heard my footsteps on the front path. Their aviary looked empty.

"Harli? Peeki?" I called. From inside the nest box that the couple shared, I heard a muffled, "Harli! Harli!" I felt a mixture of relief and excitement. Since it was not their regular bedtime, there could be only one explanation for the lorikeets' being inside the box. After all this time, Harli and Peeki were going to have babies. They'd been at Pandemonium for seven years and had never laid eggs. I'd wondered whether perhaps they were older birds and no longer fertile when they came to us, but there was no way of knowing. Then I saw the note on the counter from Angelica, the very capable woman who had cared for them in my absence.

It said that Harli had died the previous day. But hadn't Harli just spoken to me from her box? I was devastated and mystified. I called Angelica. All she could tell me was that she had found a dead lorikeet on the floor of the aviary and had taken the body to the vet for a necropsy, since this is our standard procedure.

She was fairly sure that Harli was the one who had died, but since she had hastily wrapped the body in a plastic bag, she couldn't be totally sure.

I didn't dare disturb whichever bird remained in the nest box if it was indeed sitting on eggs. Harli and Peeki were different species of lorikeet, and their markings made it easy to tell them apart. If the surviving bird didn't come out of the box, the mystery as to which had died would be solved when we got the necropsy report. The one thing that the necropsy always determines with total accuracy is the bird's sex.

The surviving bird stayed in the box and didn't come out until after dark to eat. I figured that it had to be Harli, since she was the only one of the two who talked, and the bird in the box answered, "Harli! Harli!" when I called out. The voice lacked Harli's vitality, but that was to be expected, since she'd just been widowed.

The necropsy report arrived on the day that the surviving lorikeet finally left the nest box in daylight. There was no egg, and it was Peeki who emerged. I was certain of that, since Harli was a Swainson's green-naped subspecies and had a chest that was a brighter orange than Peeki's. I opened the report; it listed the probable cause of death as botulism, possibly from spoiled food. This finding meant that the bird's death was probably avoidable. We are very careful with all feedings for individual species. In hot weather, the lorikeets' nectar can go bad, so we always take it away after four hours. The person who had been responsible for feeding the lorikeets was experienced and reliable. It was hard for me to believe that she had not put out fresh nectar. Besides, both birds had been given the same food, and only one died. Yet something had gone wrong. I had to accept that human error was most likely the cause of Harli's demise.

There was another shock in the report. The dead lorikeet was a male. This didn't make sense, since Peeki, our male, was still alive. I was perplexed. Harli *must* have been a female, since the pair had been so loving, so devoted to each other. Then I realized that I'd overlooked the most logical explanation for two male birds' having a close and loving relationship. The lorikeets could have been a contented same-sex couple. "Gay" behavior in birds wasn't unprecedented.

Two recently famous pairs of bonded male penguins in Madrid and Toronto zoos drew vastly different reactions from zoologists. Gentoo penguins named Inca and Rayas built nests together every spring at a Madrid zoo, ever hopeful despite the fact that their nests remained empty. Finally the zoo arranged for a fertilized gentoo egg from a zoo in China to be given to the pair to incubate. In Toronto, Buddy and Pedro were ultimately separated and put into enclosures with females, causing a public outcry. The zoo's reasoning: as a couple, the male penguins made an insufficient contribution to the gene pool.

Scientists studying Laysan albatross on the northwest coast of Oahu reported female couples that engaged in all the behavior that heterosexual albatross couples do—except copulating.

In the same article detailing the albatross study, the *New York Times* reported that some sort of sexual behavior in same-sex animal couples has been observed in over 450 species. I wouldn't know or care what Harli and Peeki did in the privacy of their nesting box; I do know that given both of their long, difficult journeys, life was beautiful once they shared the same perch.

After Peeki left his mourning place in the nest box, he was a changed bird, but not in ways I would have expected. Instead of retreating, he became more like Harli had been. He spoke now—in Harli's Jersey accent. I wanted to find him another partner, but I was confused. I explained my dilemma to Tom. "Which do I get? A female or a male?" If Peeki was gay, I wanted to provide him with a suitable new partner. I could find a male lorikeet, but how would I find a gay one?

And what if Peeki was straight and had adapted to being housed with a male? This was also "normal" behavior in the bird kingdom. In this case, maybe I should find a female lorikeet. Or maybe Peeki was bisexual.

Tom's suggestion was to leave it to fate. I should send word out that I was looking for a lorikeet and see what was available. It took about four months. Then I heard that a presumed-to-be-female rainbow lorikeet had been turned in to the local bird rescue.

When the new adoptee arrived, Peeki named her: "*Harli!*"

I amended it to Harli II. When I'd introduced her, Peeki had not given her the same immediate reception he'd given the original Harli; in fact, he completely ignored Harli II for a couple of months. Finally I noticed the two playing together in the birdbath. Their relationship lacked the spirit and vitality of the first pairing, but they got on reasonably well. I didn't know for sure whether Harli II was male or female, but I felt that this lorikeet was not the perfect one for Peeki and decided to keep my feelers out for another.

A year passed, and it was time for the aviculture conference again. As much as I longed to go, the memory of what I had come home to a year earlier made me think I should skip it. Tom urged me to go again; he had heard so much excitement in my voice when I had called home from the first one. I'd had the chance to visit with bird curators from zoos, query bird-food manufacturers about changes in formulation, and meet field researchers involved in saving birds in the wild. I shouldn't make decisions out of fear. After all, Harli might have died even if I hadn't been away.

I went and had a wonderful, enriching two days, but anxiety sent me home a day early. The first greeting I heard was, "Harli! Harli!" The call was much louder and more insistent than usual. I dropped my bag and ran to see what was wrong. When I'd left, Peeki and Harli II had looked fine. They had been spending more time than usual in their nest box, but I assumed that was because it was still winter and they were escaping the cold. It was almost dark out, and I could barely see. I reached inside our front door and turned on the lights to the Lorikeet Lair.

"Harli! Harli! Harli!"

Peeki was screaming louder than I'd ever heard him. I peered into the aviary, expecting the worst.

There were four lorikeets inside. My first thought was that someone had left two lorikeets without asking me if I would take them. This happened sometimes. But a closer look revealed that two of the birds were juveniles. One looked exactly like Peeki and the other like Harli II. Lorikeets incubate their eggs for thirty days, and then it takes another thirty days for the babies to fledge. There must have been babies in the nest before I'd left for the conference, but I'd had no idea.

I still miss being greeted by the first Harli every time I walk the path to my front door. But it's plenty lively in the Lorikeet Lair. Peeki now talks a lot. His vocabulary includes most of the words that our first Harli used, but he has added some phrases of his own, including "Good food!" and "Hi, there!" The family has grown in number and vocal power. Mom, Dad, and three rambunctious kids all scream out, "Harli! Harli! Harli!" every morning. I'm sure that the original Harli would find it a hoot and outscream them all.

# TEN

# Tico: The Bird Lady Gets Schooled

Five years after our first visit to the Browns', a colorful village of aviaries had arisen, taking up most of the back and side yards. They were painted in soothing tropical blues, greens, and yellows, trimmed with cupolas, trellising, and mosaics by local artists, and hung with sculptures and fountains. The donkeys added a bit of barnyard flavor, joined by a couple of darling Nigerian dwarf goats that I'd given Tom for his birthday. We seemed to be at full multispecies capacity, so when I confessed that I had been longing for a bird of my own, Tom's face took on the slack, rubbery look best described by that odd, expressive word: flabbergasted.

He recovered sufficiently to speak. "Michele, you have more than one hundred birds."

"But they're aviary birds. They have each other. I want a bird like Amigo."

"Amigo hates us both. You want a bird like that?"

Tom had a point. Amigo had never warmed to anyone but Nick and the occasional attractive female visitor, to whom he'd blurt out, "I love you!"

"I want a bird who will be a real companion. I'd like to have the type of relationship with a bird that Nick has with Amigo."

I heard a familiar sigh. Tom said he had just one request. "Please find a bird that will not call me names."

I agreed quickly, knowing that I'd really have no control over the situation. If a parrot names a human, that becomes the person's name, be it silly, unsuitable, or profane. Parrots set their own rules—a lesson I was about to relearn over and over again.

Some months passed. I knew that I couldn't go searching for such a bird. It would have to choose me, the way Amigo set his little cap for Nick. It might take a while, since I was no longer in close contact with as many adoptable birds. I had cut out my volunteer work at the humane society. Being on-site resulted in too many new occupants for our aviaries: pheasants, chukar, and still more doves. Plus, it was counterproductive to spend hours feeding birds and cleaning cages there when I had so much of the same kind of work at home with all our adoptees.

"Please help us," came the call from a shelter one day. "We're shorthanded for feeding baby birds." Well, who can resist babies? I packed a tuna sandwich and went to dropper-feed rescued hatchlings. Time does fly when frantic, relentless little beaks peep commandingly: Feed me! Feed me! After a few hours I was ravenous myself. I was heading toward the employee picnic benches for a lunch break when I heard a voice I didn't recognize.

"Come here! Come here!"

The calling continued. There was no one around, but maybe someone needed help. I followed the sound to an office door down the hall.

"Come here! Come here!"

Inside the small office, beside a desk, was a large birdcage containing a magnificent blue and gold macaw. He was about a foot and a half tall, with glossy blue-green feathers, a saffron-colored belly, and black-and-white stripes running across his cheeks. He was clinging to the side bars of his cage, swaying rhythmically back and forth. It looked as if he was dancing.

"You are *gorgeous*," I whispered. I spoke in hushed tones, afraid that I had entered an off-limits area, since the office belonged to security personnel. I was holding my tuna sandwich. The macaw eyed it, looked at me, and then looked back at the food.

"Yum!" he said.

I knew it was wrong to feed someone else's animal, but he was so insistent.

"Yum, yum!"

I offered him a crust of bread, which he reached for and downed with gusto. When he was finished, he stretched his body up tall, did his swaying dance move, and hollered, "Some more!"

The enraptured human obeyed. And thus began my behavior modification engineered by a bird brain more cunning than Batman's archrival, the Penguin.

"Yum, *yum*!"

After a few more shared morsels, I went back to my lunch and the baby-bird detail. But in the days that followed, the big macaw invaded my dreams. I'd hear him calling, Come here! Come here! The dreams were intense enough to wake me. I had the strong sensation that I needed to save this bird. In those recurring scenarios, I was always too late. I'd burst into the office and find an empty cage.

When I asked about the backroom macaw, I was told that his future was bleak. He was as dangerous as he was charming. He was kept isolated in the security office like some unexploded bomb. The big, curved beak of the macaw species had evolved strong enough to snap a Brazil nut or a two-inch-diameter branch in the wild. He lured his victims with that beseeching "Come here!" inviting them close enough to inflict a nasty bite. Nothing was known about his past. He had been left in a cardboard box in front of the shelter in the dead of night, with no information enclosed. The person who left him clearly wanted to off-load the bird fast—and without a trace of ownership. He was unadoptable, miserable, and a liability to the shelter. Sound familiar?

I knew from our experience with Amigo that so-called attack parrots probably had good reasons for their biting habits.

Baby parrots, called bappies, explore with their beaks and tongues—not unlike the generations of puppies that have gnawed on my fingers. Some bites are purely accidental. The parrot is securing his balance by putting his beak around the owner's fingers. If the person pulls away quickly, a deep cut can result. The best way to handle a beak closed on a finger is to push inward or use the other hand to carefully open the beak.

In adult parrots, some causes of biting are readily understandable to humans: fear, pain (from abuse, neglect, or undiagnosed illness), hormonal flare-ups in adolescent birds, dominance issues. More puzzling to parrot owners is the premeditated sort of "sport" biting that this macaw engaged in, sweetly enticing his victim, then doing a short victory dance once he'd hit home. Parrots' biting humans, even beloved humans, is so common that there is a lively support industry of parrot trainers and whisperers. There are plenty of sensible ways to curb a biting habit—if you have the courage and patience to stick it out.

One crucial fact unknown to most new parrot owners is that parrots adore their own noise, along with any reciprocal racket from other birds or humans. Yell at them for shrieking, and they will scream louder at the encouragement. Shout "ouch" when bitten, and they'll be tickled pink and eager to try it again. To a parrot, a loud, emotional response—even if you turn the air blue with the vilest of curses—is the equivalent of applause and calls for an encore performance. The sooner you learn that and show little or no reaction to biting behavior, the sooner your fingers will heal.

I put in an application to adopt the handsome, fierce macaw. Yep—fools rush in. I had never adopted a companion "big bird" before. This guy was five times the size of Amigo and stoked with far more aggression. It was daunting, but I felt compelled to deliver him—as best I could—from such deep misery. He was too magnificent an animal to spend what was left of his life in the equivalent of a jail cell. I told the family about submitting the application but didn't go into detail beyond, "Oh, just another parrot."

While I waited for the required inspection of our home to be scheduled, I visited the bird. Daily. When he caught sight of me, he always commanded, "Come here!" As I approached his cage, he'd dance. I brought offerings of nuts and grapes. He was a complete gentleman in the way he took the treats through the bars. This is my bird, I thought to myself. I need to get him out of this place so that he can walk around, get some exercise, some fresh air.

One day I was whispering to him and sliding small pieces of apple through the bars of his cage. He listened intently to my voice, his eyes riveted on me while he ate the apple slice. Neither of us realized that a man was standing at the door until he spoke and startled us both.

"I'm Dick. I'm the president of this outfit. And you are . . . ?"

I explained the situation, telling him that I came every day to visit this blue and gold and loved the bird, but that I wasn't sure if I'd ever be able to take him home because, nearly a month past my application, the inspection was still pending. Within fifteen minutes, I was okayed to have the macaw as a foster bird. If the home visit went well, it would be a permanent adoption. I cried with relief, thinking that the bad dreams and the bird's solitary confinement were almost at an end. Dick misinterpreted my tears for worry.

"The home visit is just a formality," he reassured me. "If the inspector finds something wrong, we'll work with you to fix it. That bird is yours."

Then he confirmed the subtext of all those nightmares: there had been lively debate on euthanizing the macaw, and soon. "No bird is going to be put to death on my watch," Dick told me. "Be good to him and he'll be the most faithful friend you'll ever have."

SO BEGAN AN epic test of wills, a contest of "who's schooling whom" so antic and intense that my friends and family actually kept score. It especially amused my sister Lynn, who is a veterinarian in Atlanta. She called often for updates. Some days the process was downright bloody, until I learned the macaw body language that signaled an imminent bite. Most of the time it was just comical, and I was the prime patsy.

The bird began his campaign for dominance the moment I

unlatched the carrier I had brought him home in. I didn't have the confidence to touch him yet, so my plan was to put the carrier inside the large cage that was to be his home. I'd open the carrier, then quickly withdraw my hand and close the bigger cage. He'd stay there for a few days, and then we'd see. But the bird had his own plan. I barely had time to pull my hand away from the carrier latch before he burst out of the carrier, beak open in attack mode, eyes glaring. I fled. There was no time to close the cage door. He stepped out, used his beak and claws to climb to the top, and looked down at me like some sort of gaudy-feathered Godzilla. He paced back and forth menacingly, every inch the monster psittacine he was reputed to be.

"How's the new bird?" Tom asked when he came home that evening. I stammered something noncommittal, but by that first day, I had all but admitted defeat to myself. Any attempt to handle this macaw would result in my getting badly hurt. I'd been able to shut him in the cage only when he went in to eat and drink. I hadn't intended a caged life for this bird. I had envisioned him a fairly free-ranging household presence, like Amigo.

Tom's question about the "new bird" got me thinking. I didn't even know the macaw's name. Doubtless he had one that he answered to. I would need to guess it. I had approximated stray animals' names before by reading aloud from a book of baby names. I'd watch the animal's reaction. Using this technique, I'd been able to come close to guessing the right name three times with lost dogs I'd rescued—or at least the dogs seemed comfortable with my approximations. I figured that a bird would react to his name just as a dog did, so I pulled out the baby-names book, sat a safe distance from the cage, and started to read out loud. I began with the *z*'s and worked my way backward.

After a few minutes, the bird became intrigued; he seemed to listen intently as I read. When he reacted to a name by breaking into a dance or becoming animated, I put a check mark in the book. My "progress" was quickly undone; the names he liked one day were not the same ones he liked the next. But he did seem to enjoy my reading to him in a soft voice. By day three, I could sit right next to his cage. By day four, right after I had opened the book, he manipulated the lock on his cage and climbed out.

Fear and shock prickled across the back of my neck as I watched him advance. The bird had been playing me—he could have escaped anytime despite the fact that I'd "locked" him in. It's possible he needed the security of being in the cage just as much as I needed him inside it. He stunned me further by climbing into my lap. I tried not to panic and focused on reading. He listened for a few minutes, then took the book out of my hands and tossed it on the floor. I had just read the name "Tico."

"Tico it is!"

It would do, anyhow. Over the next couple of weeks, I

maintained a healthy alertness around Tico, and my fear of the big macaw decreased with familiarity. Our getting-acquainted period was certainly a roller-coaster ride, though. I could never gauge his moods. Tensions came to a head when I had to take Tico to a vet for the physical exam required for final adoption. The shelter had arranged an appointment with Anne Calloway.

That first day, Tico saw this wonderful vet as the devil incarnate. He was also furious with me. It had been sheer hell to get him to the clinic; during the short drive he clung to the front bars of his carrier, swinging back and forth with a mad, menacing glare. Was I dumping him as the others had? Just another human Judas? I was as keyed up as Tico when we were shown into an examination room. Would he explode out of the carrier when we got there? As soon as I let him out, he paced the floor with great agitation. Like most of the companion birds we've adopted, he'd had his flight feathers clipped. It was heartrending to watch his panic.

"*Love* macaws!" Anne said. She talked softly to Tico. "It's okay, I'm not going to hurt you." In a trice, she had the big guy in her arms, wrapped firmly like a blue and gold burrito. "Let me be the bad guy," she said, suggesting that I stay behind while she took him to another room to clip his nails. The screams started as soon as they left, and escalated to an astonishing volume. I ran down the hall and saw them through the treatment-room glass. Tico, wrapped in a towel, was screeching murder most foul. Anne hadn't even begun treatment. I went back to wait.

When Anne came back with him, Tico was still wrapped in a towel but wringing wet. She had sprayed him with water to cool him down. And despite the drama, the vet was calm and smiling. "I love spirited birds," she said. "You have quite a honey here."

As she unwrapped Tico, he leaped into my arms, clung to my chest like an infant, and tucked his head under my chin. He was mine after all. And his behavior was ringing some primal bell. Wasn't his emotional intelligence that of a two- or three-year-old? And hadn't I seen some terrifying displays of toddler separation anxiety? It wasn't personal; it was blind, undiluted terror. I held Tico close and felt him relax.

After that, I was confident that our relationship was solid and that we would pass the home inspection for final adoption. We got no dispensation because our home was a bird sanctuary; rules are rules. When the day came, my gentleman bird ignored the strawberry the inspector had brought him and took a savage bite out of my thumb: I hoped she hadn't seen, and I stanched the bleeding as best I could, hand behind my back. A short while later, the inspector said, "Congratulations. You have a parrot."

Later, when Tico showed himself to be ungovernable around certain visitors, I became hypervigilant for more seemingly un-provoked attacks. I think I understood the message: Don't even think of giving me away to this person. You're mine, so behave.

This was a critical attitude adjustment for me. I surely didn't "own" the maverick Tico, but parrots do have very proprietary attitudes toward a favored human. It was far more complicated than the simple, loving relationships I'd had with so many dogs and cats. The ups and downs with Tico continued to be baffling and frustrating; he'd be a snuggle bunny one day, angry and distant the next. I realize now that my understanding was limited by my viewpoint. If Tico wanted to chew on a toy instead of coming out of his cage to be petted, I judged him aloof. If I insisted on making him leave his activity in order to play with me, his open beak seemed aggressive to me.

The real message was, Stay away, I want to play by myself now. After all, from Tico's point of view, I belonged to *him*. When he wanted to play with me, he'd call. And if I didn't heed his summons at once—maybe I'd been off running an errand—an angry bird would lunge at me through his cage when I finally approached, beak poised for retribution, as if to say, Where have you been? How dare you leave me?

Recognizing the basic cues of a toddler tantrum, I had strategies to avoid them. One method I used with Tico was just to pretend not to notice how peeved he was. Combined with bribery, it worked pretty consistently. I'd see an agitated parrot glaring at me and whisper praises and apologies. "Oh my, how beautiful you look today. I am so sorry to have left you alone. Here, I brought you a treat." I'd put on music, start to dance and act silly. Before long, Tico would forget he was furious with me, and we would dance.

As the months passed, I gathered a few clues about Tico's past life. He had an odd way of putting himself to sleep at night. I would sit out of sight and listen. There was a period of loud, persistent hacking that sounded like an old woman with smoker's cough, seriously unwell. Then came her laughter, a pitch-perfect cackle befitting a lady of a certain age, sounding utterly delighted—perhaps by her brilliant bird. It seemed to me that the nightly ritual afforded Tico some sort of comfort and let him drift off to sleep. I think that he may have been well loved and was traumatized by his owner's death. In fear and grief, he may have lashed out at any relative or executor and was consequently dumped at the shelter.

Anyone who has worked in animal rescue or adopted a stray knows the questions that arise when you watch abnormal or aggressive behavior in an abandoned creature: Who did this to you? What can we do to make it stop hurting?

WHATEVER TICO'S BACKSTORY, I knew that I had a smart and cunning bird who now liked me well enough. I got cocky and thought I'd teach him a few tricks. I planned to start with getting him to give a simple high five when I lifted my right palm up near his left shoulder.

The first session started casually. I played with Tico while he was standing on a perch. If he lifted his left foot, I'd touch my palm to the bottom of his foot, say clearly, "High five!" and reward him with his favorite treat, a sunflower seed. It seemed to go well after a few repeats. Realizing he could earn a treat, Tico responded to my signal every time. Once I was sure that Tico had "captured the behavior," in training parlance, I ended the session.

Tico wanted more sunflower seeds and raised his foot. But I was already walking away. He loosed a piercing shriek and kept it up—at an excruciating volume. Even bird-loving Nick moaned, "Mom, the parrot is hurting my ears!" Tom begged me to make him stop. So I did the expedient thing and shoved a whole handful of sunflower seeds to keep Tico busy as I made a getaway. A really big treat is called a jackpot by animal trainers. It is a way to show that you really, really like what the animal has done.

Over the next few days, Tico reinforced my training—at top volume—and wallowed gleefully in his jackpots. Two or three times a day he raised his foot when he saw me looking at him. If I didn't bribe him with sunflower seeds, he would scream and drive the family nuts. I worried that they might even pressure me to move Tico's cage to a less central place in the house, just as we were becoming acquainted. I had captured the behavior my eighteen-inch trainer intended: Foot up? Give Tico a treat. On the double!

You'd think I might gracefully accept defeat. But I respected Tico's intelligence enough to put it to another test. Above all, I wanted to keep him stimulated. At a bird show, I had seen birds that could identify shapes and colors, a skill they demonstrated by fitting puzzle pieces into matching holes. I ordered a plastic puzzle meant for birds and bought a couple of inexpensive children's wooden puzzles on eBay. The plastic one arrived first. I put Tico and the package on a table. He was very interested in the paper and tape and had great fun ripping up the cardboard box. He refused to go near the puzzle.

After many tries, I got Tico to pick up a puzzle piece and drop it. He treated it as though it were carrion, touching as little of it as possible, then quickly dropping it. Once he was given a food reward, he would race to the far end of the table, climb on the back of a chair, and break out a few dance moves that seemed to declare, This foolishness is beneath me. Wooden puzzles irritated him more; he would pick up a piece, then fling it as far as he could.

Even though neither of us enjoyed these sessions, I kept it up and got no rewards for my stubbornness. When my sister Lynn called, she asked how the lessons were going. "Not well," I confessed. "I may have to stop soon because I keep losing pieces." The acrylic ones had been the first to go; only three of the initial seven pieces were left. I had switched to just the wooden puzzles, but those pieces had gone missing as well. I told Lynn, "It's just as well. He doesn't seem to be smart enough to figure out that after you pick up a piece, you're supposed to drop it in the corresponding slot."

She tried to be consoling. "Wow, I guess birds are like humans. Some are smarter than others." A few days later, I was at the computer in my office, and Tico was on a stand beside me. I left for a moment, and Tico didn't notice my return. I watched him from the doorway. He had left the perch and was walking toward my bookcase. He climbed up, using his beak and feet to pull himself to the next shelf, and when he reached the third shelf, where I kept the puzzles, he picked up a yellow square from the plastic set, climbed down, walked to the trash basket, and dropped the piece in.

Game, set, and match—Tico!

It was challenging enough to go mano a mano with this guy, but when he enlisted some other companion birds in his pranks, I was nearly undone. It was summertime, when the parrots live in outdoor aviaries. Tico's gang of three consisted of himself, Amigo, and a foster Indian ringneck named Kiwi. Their aviaries were beside one another. I went out to visit with them and found Tico in Amigo's aviary and Amigo in Tico's. I thought I'd put the parrots in the wrong place. A few days later, I found Tico, Kiwi, and Amigo all in the same aviary instead of their separate ones. I suspected that one of my children was playing a trick on me. Next I found Tico in Kiwi's aviary, Amigo in his own roost, and Kiwi outside, standing atop her aviary. A red-tailed hawk circled overhead. It could have easily snatched the tempting ringneck.

The human reconsidered. Tico did not like Kiwi. Tico had the motive, he had the opportunity, and he had the skill at opening cage doors. What I hadn't realized until that moment was that he could also close doors behind him and look utterly innocent. I quickly returned the birds to their own cages, and that afternoon I bought a combination padlock to put on Tico's door.

At first he seemed intrigued. He likes all kinds of hardware as long as it's real. He disdains parrot toys. Since keeping parrots physically and intellectually engaged is essential to their well-being, a huge market has developed for intriguing bird toys. I had noticed one advertised on the Web that consisted of a steel wheel with complex nuts and bolts in it. It was expensive, but I decided it would be perfect for Tico and I ordered one. He refused to touch it. The next morning I found the toy on the ground. Tico had managed to unscrew the stainless steel bolts I'd used to hang it from a beam in the roof.

The cage padlock did thwart Tico. But I had problems with it, too. The numbers on it were small, my fingers were often cold and clumsy on chilly mornings, and I sometimes forgot the combination. After a few days, I took to leaving the lock on, but unlocked; I doubted that Tico could tell the difference.

This gave me a false sense of security, and I assumed all was well.

I should have known better. By then our sons were teenagers and liable to be just as crafty as Tico, sneaking out of the house after curfew with the same daredevil stealth. Once, they threw a party while Tom and I were away, and they did such a good job cleaning up afterward that we had no idea what they'd been up to—until I found the recycling bin full of empty beer bottles. He began sneaking out for some fun in the garden, creeping back home, and shutting the door with the unlocked padlock swinging from the handle just as I'd left it. Tico's smoking gun: a mess of broken branches and chewed-up, mangled leaves surrounding his aviary. Busted!

I managed to keep him contained after that, but I was out of my league with this guy and ordered a parrot-training manual. The instructions seemed rudimentary. You ignored behaviors that were undesirable and rewarded those that you liked. The book suggested that you identify which behaviors you wanted to extinguish and which you wanted to reinforce. I followed the suggestion that I write down my goals, along with a plan. It went like this:

*Goal:*

1. Extinguish Tico's "Come here" when he wants to bite someone.
2. Teach Tico to say "Come here" when he wants me to transport him.

*Plan:*

> Ignore him when he screams; go to him only when
> he is quiet or talking softly. When I pick him up, say
> gently, "Come here."

It looked good on paper. Tico, alas, would not be ignored. He just screamed louder. When this failed to bring me to him, he developed an alternate training plan, drawn from his own crafty manual. Instead of screaming, he would mess further with me by using animal calls. Doubtless he had noticed me responding to distress calls from our other animals. Tico is a fabulous mimic.

He tried a coyote howl first. A coyote visit is not a welcome event at any time, but to hear one howl in daytime is alarming, since only a sick or starving coyote would venture close to the house before dark. When I heard the coyote near Tico's outdoor cage one afternoon, I grabbed a broom and rushed outside to shoo it away. Tico watched the slapstick, celebrated with a few quick Travolta/Latin hustle turns, and then stretched out his right foot—his cue for wanting to be picked up. I doomed myself by laughing. I couldn't help it. And dutifully, I brought my bad boy inside the house. Again, Tico had captured the behavior he wanted from me. I was well on my way to being trained to come to Tico on command.

The coyote howls went on; I ignored them. Then I heard the "mehhhh" of our little goats coming from the wrong part of the yard. There went my flowerbeds, if the goats had escaped their pen. Again I charged outside. *Tico.* Next, there were donkeys braying far away from their corral. Out I went; score another for the bird. Dogs were clamoring to come in. But wait—the dogs were all inside. Gotcha, smart guy. I stayed put, and Tico doubled down.

Distress calls were his next ploy. I heard what sounded like Minx, our cat, in a feline brawl and rushed outside. There was only Tico, doing his victory dance and stretching out that right foot. I didn't pick him up, but I couldn't hold back the grin. Then, during another phone call with my sister Lynn, I heard our old dog Shannon whining outdoors. In her final years, Shannon was blind and regularly got lost in our backyard. Her voice had become hoarse, and instead of barking, she whined with a distinctive distress call when she needed to be rescued.

"Got to run. Shannon needs help," I told my sister. "Call you later."

"Michele!" Lynn yelled into the phone before I could hang up. "Shannon is dead! You're probably hearing Tico."

She was right. The bird had driven me out where the buses don't run. I was hearing dead dogs.

"Chalk up another for the parrot," crowed my sister.

I can admit it now: I enjoy matching wits with Tico even if I am always the one wearing egg on my face. I'm sure this is because the big, scary macaw had indeed become my darling—the best of dancers during our morning boogaloo sessions, and an absolute love when the mood struck him. He would nestle close, with his head under my chin. I spoke to him only in soft, quiet tones—something I've learned works best for all our birds, thanks to observing its effects on Tico. We danced most mornings. I let him lead, of course.

And then I was jilted. For a vain if beautiful airhead named Mylie. Like many of our other parrots, she was adopted from Mickaboo, a companion-bird rescue group in the Bay Area. I had met one of the volunteers in Anne's waiting room during Tico's first visit there, and I was impressed by the group's knowledge and dedication. Mylie is a rescued Catalina macaw, a hybrid produced only in captivity by breeding a blue and gold macaw, like Tico, with the magnificent scarlet macaw. She has a bright yellow chest, a blue-green head, and an elegant, tapered tail.

At that point, most of our parrots were in a large outdoor aviary together. Once I introduced Mylie to the flock, Tico fell hard for the comely and colorful newcomer, who didn't vocalize much more than "kiss, kiss." Soon they were a bonded pair, their connection tight and exclusive.

No more snuggling with Tico for me. Very little dancing. More biting? You bet. Probably had to do with hormones, and it's also about monogamous love. The two are insistent that they not be separated even for their morning transfer to the outdoor aviaries. We now use wooden perches rather than our tempting hands to transport them, and they like to share a perch for their trip outside in the morning, and then back inside in the evening. They spend their days together preening and communing in parrotspeak. I do wish Tico had chosen a mate of his own intelligence. But Mylie is the beauty queen that knocked him witless, and it's okay. Their mutual devotion has resulted in a quality of life that's a main objective in rescue. I dearly miss "my" bird. But the past is irrelevant if their future is assured.

Mia Bird, *African gray parrot*

Peeki, *rainbow lorikeet*

Scarlet-chested grass parakeet

Mylie, *Catalina macaw*

*Rosy Bourke parakeets*

*Plum-headed parakeet*

*Vulturine Guinea fowl*

*Nicobar pigeon*

Ferguson, *East African crowned crane*

*"The Last Aviary"* at Pandemonium Aviaries

# ELEVEN

#  Hello, Pretty Mama

I'd say that by now I might qualify as an avian psycho-therapist—if our birds didn't continue to surprise and confound me with their range and expressions of feeling. Birds are deep. Human understanding of their emotional needs is inadequate at best.

It is a pretty widespread assumption that animals do mourn, and intensely. Some wrenching evidence went viral in August of 2011. Millions of people worldwide were moved by the photo of Hawkeye, a Labrador retriever who refused to budge from beneath the flag-draped coffin of his Navy SEAL handler Jon Tumilson, killed when his helicopter was shot down in Afghanistan. It's almost impossible not to choke up at the image of the bereaved black dog stretched limply on a chill marble floor.

No one has to convince me that some animals feel profoundly, given what I've seen. There is plenty of scientific literature and anecdotal evidence to show that animals in the wild mourn their own, often with something humans might classify as ritual. A much-viewed *National Geographic* video shows elephants encircling and "respecting" their dead; crow and magpie "funerals" have been examined in scholarly journals and in the amazing book *Gifts of the Crow,* by John Marzluff and Tony Angell. They also write a fascinating blog for *Psychology Today* called *Avian Einsteins,* which explores bird intelligence and emotions.

I wish that providing a balm for avian grief could always be as simple as finding the bird a new mate. That's often a viable solution with our aviary birds. But there is nothing as straightforward for helping companion birds whose emotional turmoil is tied to their previous relationships with humans. Where do you begin to try to ease the screaming night terrors of a sweet parrot whose doting owners simply gave her away after twenty-two years? What does a one-legged Lady Ross's turaco who has hidden in a cardboard box much of his life require—and does his connection to autistic boys come out of his own traumatic past? The origins of a rescued companion bird's behavioral tics are almost always a mystery, since most of these birds come to us from shelters or rescue organizations with scant or no histories and plenty of issues. When the adoption is direct—that is, when I'm contacted by people who cannot or will not keep their birds—I may have a bit more to go on. But the reserves of guilt and deception about off-loading an animal often cloud the truth. Lying or withholding information only hurts the chances of a good readjustment.

If compassion is the essence of a rescue organization, summoning forgiveness for human transgressions is the much tougher job requirement. It still appalls me when people just walk away with little thought or preparation for the animal's future life. The need for accountability is best expressed in a quote from Antoine de Saint-Exupéry's famous children's fable, *The Little Prince.* The title character in the book befriends a wild fox. "Many have forgotten this truth, but you must not forget it. You remain responsible, forever, for what you have tamed."

When Amadeus, the Lady Ross's turaco, arrived at Pandemonium, it was supposed to be a temporary arrangement. For four years, until it proved too problematic, I took birds in a foster care program when their owners were too ill or financially unstable to care for them; if and when the situation improved, the birds went back home. I did not charge for their care.

The woman who brought Amadeus left six other exotic birds with us; I had helped her find homes for seven more. Her house was "underwater" financially and she was forced into a short sale and a move to temporary housing that did not allow animals of any kind. She hoped to reclaim her birds when she got back on her feet. I agreed to take the ones that were hardest to place. Amadeus fit that category because he was handicapped and, as a result, emotionally crippled—at least according to his owner.

Turacos are fruit-eating birds from sub-Saharan Africa. They are arboreal, flitting swiftly through the tree canopy. At Pandemonium, where we now have three species of turacos, we provide them bird-safe, sturdy manzanita branches and feed them papayas, apples, and blueberries, along with vitamin and mineral pellets.

Amadeus is a striking bird with a missing leg. His head feathers are bright crimson and stick straight up, and his beak is bright yellow, somewhat reminiscent of a duck's, but slimmer. His body is covered in sleek, shiny black feathers everywhere except on the head and under the wings, where patches glow red when he flies. His color comes from real pigment, which is unique to turacos. In most bird species, feather color is a result of the refraction of light on the feather shaft rather than of intrinsic, chemically based pigmentation, as in turacos.

When I asked how Amadeus had lost his leg, the owner's explanation was cursory and puzzling. She had come home from work one day and found the turaco with a broken leg. She had no idea how it had happened. A vet put a cast on it, but when the cast was removed, the entire leg "fell off." It seemed strange. When I asked about his personality, I was told, "He's very shy, very quiet. Never vocalizes. Make sure he always has a cardboard box so that he can hide in it. As long as he has a hiding place, he'll be fine."

She assured me that I could put all seven birds that I was fostering for her in the same aviary, since she had done so. I wasn't convinced this was a good idea, because the other birds were all grain eaters and were a lot more nimble than one-legged Amadeus. After a day of watching Amadeus hang back while the other birds got first dibs at feeding time, I decided that my suspicions were correct; he got a chance to eat only after the other birds were finished and the fruit meant for him had long disappeared. I had just separated the aviary that abuts the house into two components. One was for the lorikeets and had Plexiglas panels around it; the other was empty and perfect for Amadeus. I could keep close tabs on this supposedly shy bird right through the dining room window. I also made him special perches for his handicap and gave him a hideaway box for that alleged shyness. He never used it.

Once Amadeus was in an aviary alone, he became one of the most social and vocal birds I'd ever met. And loud. Since he could see the front walk, he became our welcome bird. Before a visitor even had a chance to ring the doorbell, Amadeus would belt out a joyous greeting: "*Who, whoooo! Who, whoooo.*" We all fell hard for our disabled turaco. Then his owner returned to claim him. Her life had stabilized and she intended to get her birds back. Amadeus was at the top of her list.

She arrived to retrieve him with a woman she described as her "bird nanny," a seemingly lovely and gracious person who had cared for the owner's birds when she traveled. The woman was quite knowledgeable; she spoke kindly to all the birds in the cages that line our dining room. They responded to her calmly, as though they had known her for a while.

I was dreading the loss of a bird I'd grown so fond of. I opened the dining room window that abutted his aviary to feed him a last blueberry. He gobbled it down. I then opened the window wide enough to let him come inside so that he could be reunited with his owner. He hopped over to her but refused to take the blueberry she offered. By then she and I were both sitting on the floor with the bird between us. Amadeus hopped over to me and began sucking on my toe. She called him and offered the blueberry, but he stayed glued to my side, standing on his one foot and leaning his body against my foot. She was annoyed.

"I'll just have to towel him," she snapped.

It was inconceivable to me that anyone would have to force this genial bird to come to them, since it was always easy for me just to pick him up. Suddenly the bird nanny turned to Amadeus's owner and addressed her firmly: "If you try to take Amadeus away from here, I will throw myself in front of your car to prevent you from doing it." She turned to me and said, "Amadeus lost his leg because my friend here allowed a hornbill to live in the same aviary. Hornbills are predators. They eat birds like Amadeus. It's lucky he's still alive. I can tell he's happy. He knows he is safe here, and here is where he needs to be."

I was stunned into an uncharacteristic silence. That cardboard box. He must have silently hidden in it out of fear for his life, every day.

"Who, whoooo!"

Amadeus sang his happy hosannas as the two visitors drove off, and I was left to ponder his sudden and happy reversal of fortune. The bird nanny cared so much about Amadeus's well-being that she was willing to risk losing a friendship in order to ensure that the turaco was where he belonged, and safe.

NOT LONG AFTER, it became clear that Amadeus had a sensitivity to the silent suffering of humans who have no voice. An acquaintance and his son Chad, who was diagnosed with autism, came to visit. It was always a special interaction to watch. One particular visit by father and son was an especially moving experience for us all.

Michael and Chad passed Amadeus's aviary. The quiet was almost eerie as our noisy welcomer regarded our approach. Nary a "whooooo" escaped his beak. The bird was watching Chad intently. I opened the aviary door and pressed my body against the screening to let Chad enter past me without our touching; he did not like loud noises or body contact. He went to a folding chair I had placed in the aviary and sat motionless, his eyes staring at the ground, his hands folded on his lap. For a minute or so, there was no movement from either boy or bird.

I stepped outside the aviary and soundlessly closed the door behind me. Michael pressed close to the wire, watching Chad. His face was tight with apprehension. We both knew that if Amadeus made a fraction of his normal noise or flew near his visitor's face, Chad would have a traumatic and potentially harmful meltdown. This was their third visit, but the boy had always stayed outside the aviary.

Chad was entranced by Amadeus and had been asking for a bird of his own. His father was concerned about that. Life was already tense and complicated for this family, and adding a pet might not be the best thing to do. But as a parent willing to try almost anything to help his child, he had brought Chad again for a visit and a talk about a companion bird for him.

Amadeus seemed equally interested in Chad—enough to change his own behavior entirely. His normal greeting for any visitor is to call out loudly as he flies from branch to branch. That day with Chad, he flew down to the aviary floor and stood as still as he could manage. With only one leg, Amadeus is not comfortable standing on the floor. The only time I've seen him on the floor is when Chad visited.

After less than a minute of scrutiny, Amadeus flew to Chad's lap, using the boy's body to steady himself. Alighting anywhere is hard for Amadeus. The wide, flat perches in his aviary are wrapped in athletic tape to cushion the hard surface. Even these are challenging. Sitting on an uneven surface such as a lap is quite an athletic feat. Yet Amadeus managed it. He has sat in Chad's lap, and in the laps of other autistic boys, but never in anyone else's. Amadeus will take blueberries from my finger, sucks on my thumb, and rubs noses with me when I crouch down to look at him from eye level. But sit on my lap? Never.

Even petting him is tricky. It's difficult for him to maintain his balance if I run my fingers over his neck feathers, so I rarely try.

With these autistic boys, there is a connection that seems to stabilize both of them. Even a casual observer could not help noticing how relaxed and at peace bird and boy are when they are together. After a couple of minutes, Amadeus could no longer manage the uneven surface, so he flew off, a flash of vermilion visible underneath his wings. The boy watched as Amadeus settled on an overhead perch. He was still close to Chad but clearly finished with this interaction. Therapy session over.

This silent kinship with autistic boys doesn't seem to transfer to autistic girls, nor to any other children. Amadeus just sticks to his specialty. When Chad got up and left the aviary, Michael asked eagerly, "Did you enjoy that? Was it fun?" The boy reached toward his dad with one hand, fingers outstretched. He touched his dad's leg lightly with his fingertips, and I saw tears in Michael's eyes.

Michael asked about getting Chad a bird. Where could they find a Lady Ross's turaco? I cautioned that this might not be the best idea for several reasons. First, birds are as different from one another as humans are, and I doubted whether he would find another Lady Ross's turaco who responded like Amadeus. And then there is the messy issue of keeping a pet turaco in the house. They eat fruit like blueberries, papaya and apples. Papaya is expensive and sometimes hard to find, and because of the blueberries, turaco poop is violet colored—not so great for upholstered furniture and rugs! More important than the Technicolor dive-bombing issue, though, was how to keep this sort of bird happy. I feared it required a lot more attention than these stressed parents could manage.

They decided against a bird, and we had to end Amadeus's visit with autistic boys shortly after. He now has a breathtaking companion, a female violaceous turaco named Kenya. She is afraid of people, so we don't allow anyone into the aviary that she and Amadeus share. She has been getting calmer and more comfortable over time. She still won't take a blueberry out of my hand, but she will sit next to Amadeus when he takes one from me. He then turns his head and feeds the blueberry to Kenya.

I don't know whether Kenya will ever feel totally comfortable around people, but she and Amadeus are happy together. Their contented bonding keeps us on mission. Maybe someday Amadeus will again deploy his compassionate skills on autistic young boys of his own volition. But we'd never try to force him into the role of a "service" bird.

There is an expanding field of service-animal therapy that pairs birds, usually parrots, with people who have psychiatric and emotional disorders. The birds are carefully trained, but some, like Amadeus, seem to have natural inclinations to connect with troubled humans. In 2008, the *New York Times* reported on a fascinating relationship between an "assistance parrot" named Sadie and Jim Eggers, a Saint Louis man who described himself as bipolar "with psychotic tendencies" that have led to public rages, property destruction, and arrests. Sadie rides in a special backpack, and when she senses signs of an anger flare-up, she helps defuse the situation with a calming voice in his ear: "It's O.K., Jim. Calm down, Jim. You're all right, Jim. I'm here, Jim." Eggers got her from a friend who owned a pet store and took her in. Sadie had endured an owner so neglectful that the stressed bird had torn out most of her feathers. Eggers said the bird trained herself in the calming mode after witnessing his anger erupt at home (though it was never, ever directed at the bird). Since they'd been together, Eggers had had only one public incident, denting a woman's car fender with his fist. That day, he had left Sadie at home.

IN OUR OWN home, I was dreading a potential flare-up and some avian grieving. Nick had chosen a college in Canada. At first he thought he could bring Amigo with him, but it became clear that this was not possible. Amigo was left with his two least favorite humans: Tom and me. The parrot remained in familiar surroundings, though, with people he knew. He tolerated my taking care of him; if he needed a head scratch or wanted to be moved out of his cage, I was his only choice.

Once Nick was gone, Amigo couldn't continue to live under his bed without supervision. The first cage I got for him barely fit in Nick's room. Later, when we adopted Tico, who is much larger than Amigo, I decided to give Tico the bigger cage and I found a smaller one for Amigo. For Amigo it was a double slight. He had lost Nick and now his roost. And I was to blame for it all.

As with firstborn children who have to bear the brunt of their parents' inexperience, I had made plenty of mistakes with Amigo. And parrots don't forget. Chief among Amigo's resentments: I had refused to believe that he had really chosen Nick that day in Dr. Varner's clinic. But Amigo's vindication came a while after Nick had left for college. One day I was working in my office when a young woman, a summer intern working with the birds, walked into the office with Amigo on her shoulder. I started to scold. Carrying a parrot that way was in clear violation of the Pandemonium rules.

"It's not my fault," she explained sheepishly. "Amigo called me over, and while I was standing in front of his cage, he opened his cage door, reached over with his beak, and grabbed onto my shirt, and then climbed on me."

Amigo was already preening her hair, something he'd done only with Nick. I knew it was wrong to let him stay on anyone's shoulder, but I was also certain he wouldn't bite his new love. Then Amigo suddenly stopped running his beak through her hair.

"Why?" he asked. And since no one answered, he went on: "Why not?"

The intern giggled. Amigo launched into his old routine.

"Why? Why not? Why? Why not?"

Our philosopher-parrot was back and courting a new relationship. I closed my eyes and let myself be transported to the sweet days when I watched in wonder at how much a boy and a parrot could love each other. Finally I had to credit the little green bird with having impressive skills for assessing the human heart.

Why not?

# TWELVE

# The Flock in Peril:
# Mice, Men, and Microbes

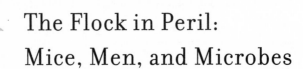

What you don't know about birds can kill them. I learned this the hard way. I also discovered a disturbing addendum: the most deadly perils may be hiding in plain sight. Our birds have weathered serious crises inflicted by disarmingly familiar creatures, from man to mouse to microbe. While all were devastating, the most disturbing was the harm done by man. A human can smile and croon that he just *adores* birds while he does his best to destroy them.

Since many of our aviaries were being added during the housing boom that ended in 2008, good carpenters were hard to find; rarer still were those we could afford. We were still financing the sanctuary ourselves on a wing, a prayer, and some serious scrimping. A few aviaries were modified garden sheds from Costco. When we realized that we had to expand yet again, the scarcity of carpenters led me to hire Ivan, a glowering, taciturn man with a mysterious knack for "finding" expensive building materials and tossing them into his truck.

Ivan sported an impressive set of upper torso tattoos. They were always on display, since he worked with his shirt off. Our son Ross, who was nine at the time, was fascinated by the well-endowed women and fierce mythical beasts that chased one another across Ivan's chest and shoulders. He spent a lot of time with Ivan.

One day Ross asked me, "Did you know that you can get a tattoo in jail?"

I admitted that I didn't.

"Well, you can. You pay for it with cigarettes and smack, although I don't understand why you smack the tattoo person."

I stopped chopping vegetables and asked him, "Where did you hear that?"

He proudly told me that his new friend Ivan was a really "rad" guy. Settling at the kitchen table, Ross spooled out some of Ivan's tales of life behind bars. The details suggested an alarming authenticity. When I told Tom about it, he was sure that if Ivan had indeed been in jail, he had probably been put away for a drug conviction or some other nonviolent crime. "Why don't you ask him why he did time?" Tom suggested.

I was wrestling with how to broach the subject when Ross piped up that he had already asked Ivan why he'd landed in jail.

"Killed a guy," Ivan had apparently told Ross. "We got in a fight and I hit him with a bottle. Went away for seven years." Then he grimly advised our son, "Don't ever drink."

For two days, Ross had refused all liquids, and now we knew why. We had gotten to the bottom of his aversion, but I was less and less comfortable having Ivan around. I was also afraid to fire him, even though he was a lousy carpenter. Nails were sticking out of places where they shouldn't, and there were large gaps between the walls and the floor and between the walls and the roof. All of it was bad for the birds. But what if he *had* killed a man? Fortunately, Ivan spared us the angst of canning him by simply disappearing one day—along with a bunch of our tools.

Looking back, I have to say he was a model citizen compared to the carpenter I hired to finish the aviary Ivan had left in pieces. I found Ron through the manager of our hardware store. "Ron is your guy," he told me, with no hint of irony or equivocation. "When you meet him, you might think he's crazy. He's not. Just a bit off, that's all."

When your house is full of yawping, pooping caged birds because you've run out of aviary space, your judgment may be clouded. After all, Ron was recommended by a trusted local merchant. And he seemed okay, if a bit strange looking. He was about five feet tall and very slim, with unruly red hair, and he dressed head to toe in army gear: tall boots, camouflage pants and shirt, all topped with a green metal helmet that harked back to the World War I doughboys.

"Were you in the armed services?" I asked, trying to break the ice. Ron was silent for several seconds. Then he nodded his head.

"Secret Service," he whispered. "Don't tell anyone. They're still after me." Ron raised his index finger to his lips and added,

"Never trust anyone. You never know who is on the side of good or"—he lowered his voice—"the side of evil."

Great—from a murderer to a conspiracy theorist. At least it seemed the lesser of personality flaws. I'll say this: Ron was a decent carpenter, but he had a maddening tic. He needed praise for his skills each time he drove in a nail. He'd call me over every few minutes: "Look, Michele! Isn't this hinge amazing?" Soon I was sneaking around my own home just to avoid bestowing the constant kudos he required.

I was crouched in the kitchen one afternoon, stealthily brewing some tea, when Ron strolled into the room. As soon as he saw me, he dropped into a squat level with mine. "I'm here. You're safe," he whispered to me. He patted his belt where his hammer hung from a strap. "No one is going to hurt you while I'm around. I'll protect you."

I got up and assured him that I was grateful for his help. I don't know why, but I asked, "Who are you protecting me from?"

"The evil ones. You know. The ones who are letting your birds out."

A dim little bell went off. I had indeed lost birds since Ron started working. First a ringneck dove went missing, then an emerald dove. I was the only person feeding and watering the birds, and none had escaped in my presence, so how and why the birds went missing was a mystery. I had found no trace of marauding raccoons or coyotes. A few days after our kitchen summit, I saw Ron standing in an aviary, filling the water dish. The door was wide open. I ran outside, shoved the door shut, and told Ron he was never to enter an occupied aviary again. "But I love birds. I want to give them fresh water," he insisted.

A couple of days later I found him inside a cage again, door open. I reiterated—strongly—that he was not to be in there, ever, and that these exotic birds would perish in the wild if they escaped. It was as if he were hearing the warning for the first time. He repeated that he loved birds—just wanted to give them water. I caught him a third time and decided that he had to go. The next day was Friday, Ron's day off. As I did errands around town, I contemplated how and when to get him off the property safely on Monday. Halfway home, a strange and sudden dread took hold of me. I felt panicky, with a painful pit in my stomach. Something felt awfully wrong. But it was Friday, so it should be okay, right?

I can't explain the premonition that pushed me to ignore the speed limit on my way home. I found Ron standing in front of the Aussie Aviary, net in hand. A male scarlet-chested grass parakeet struggled within it. I looked inside the aviary: of the thirteen birds that should have been there, only two remained, a crippled female and her fledgling, both on the ground. Neither could fly well, but the others had all taken advantage of some breach in the cage.

I saw immediately how it had happened. Along the perimeter of the aviary, right underneath the roof, there was a series of five-inch-diameter ventilation holes. A wire grate covered each of them so that the birds could not get out. Now, three of the wire grates were lying on the floor of the aviary. The screws that had held them in place were on the ground. It was clear that the grates had been purposely unfastened.

I wanted to scream. It was November and the cold winter rains had already started. There was no way these warm-climate Australian birds could survive without shelter. They had been born in captivity, so they did not have the skills to find food on their own. Their spectacular coloration would make them easy targets for predators. I stood there unable to speak coherently for a moment, but Ron was downright cheerful. He was wearing a creepy grin.

"Whew. Good thing I happened to be in the neighborhood. I saved your bird. See." He held up the net with the male scarlet-chested. It was Ben, the son of one of the birds that I'd gotten from Louis and Carol the day we'd met.

"Grates must have fallen off. Good thing I stopped by to check on the birds. If I wasn't here, you'd have lost all of them. Don't you worry, now, young lady. I'll put these grates back on, lickety-split."

I snatched the netted bird from him, and I shook as I watched him make the repair. Then I locked the aviary door myself. If I spoke to Ron, I can't recall what I might have said. I had unwittingly exposed my birds to a lying psychopath, and I'm sure I was in some sort of shock. Later, when I told Tom, I thought back to the first time we fell so hard for the scarlet-chested grass parakeets at the Browns'. These loquacious four-inch birds are among the most beautiful in the world. This was like tossing rubies into a landfill. And how badly the birds would suffer. I couldn't bear to think about it.

At first, Tom seemed circumspect about Ron's transgression. I insisted Ron had to be fired without delay. Tom countered, "There's no proof that he let the birds out. I asked him if he'd done it, and he insisted he loves birds and would never hurt them." But we both realized that the guy was unhinged. Tom spoke my worst fear aloud: Ron might be dangerous. If we fired him, he might come back and exact revenge, even hurt other birds. Tom came up with an effective plan: He paid Ron in full for the job even though it wasn't finished. He made up a story to explain why we wanted the construction to end immediately. Ron left humming.

It took me a long time to see past the horror of it; I was tormented by thoughts of those beautiful creatures dying, one by one, frightened, starving, being torn apart by predators. I walked around the house in a sort of protracted mourning, distracted and straggly haired. After a few days, Tom shook me out of it: "You're scaring the kids."

He was right. My juggling act between birds and kids had become lopsided. I owed the boys an explanation for the turmoil and for my upsetting behavior. I sat them down and presented it as an allegorical bedtime story that had a happy ending: the missing birds were thriving in the wild, with lots of babies raised in sweet, safe freedom, for ever and ever, amen. They seemed to accept it. I wish I could have. I still cling to some hope that a few of the scarlet-chested grass parakeets survived that cold, stormy winter, but I know it's highly unlikely. We have had more grass parakeets given to us and some babies born here. But I've never been able to name or get close to any of them.

IT MAY NOT be as fanciful as the over-the-rainbow ending I made up for the boys, but we did find a heaven-sent carpenter—a master craftsman who also happened to have a deep knowledge of bird keeping. It came about by accident. I had wrenched my back lifting a sack of birdseed, and the chiropractor who restored me knew of a terrific carpenter.

Actually it was a family of brothers. Johnny, the oldest, managed the projects. He had raised birds in the Philippines with his father—who had raised them with *his* father. Johnny loves and respects birds. All his crew are experts at netting birds, but Johnny also knows how to medicate, draw blood, design nest boxes, and figure out exactly where to put up perches. He is now an invaluable friend and ally. He and his crew keep all the aviaries—and my peace of mind—in very good repair.

One morning, Johnny and I were working side by side catching birds in order to give them worming medicine. I realized that I had become much, much better at netting and holding birds and that I'd learned both techniques from watching Johnny. Previously, when I had wanted to net a bird, I'd chased the bird as it flew in panic trying to get away from me. Johnny's method was to watch a bird fly for a minute or two before lifting the net and catching the bird. Birds in an aviary often become creatures of habit. If they fly from side to side in the aviary, they tend to take the same route and land in the same place, especially if the aviary is small. If you can predict where the bird will land, you can be ready to net it on that spot. When I employed Johnny's technique, I was able to net a bird much more quickly and with a lot less stress on both the bird and me. Johnny also showed me a better way to hold a bird, using his middle finger and thumb to hold onto neck bones. I followed his lead, and presto! I was able to handle even birds with sharp beaks without being bitten or overstressing the bird.

We work together at Pandemonium nearly every Saturday now, and we always talk birds. Watching Johnny's crew build and maintain safe, beautiful habitats and handle the birds with respect and skill is a blessed reassurance. The low rumble of Johnny's truck rounding the corner means the cavalry is coming, and I'm happy to open the gates.

It's not only humans like those first rogue carpenters who imperil our birds. Another great threat was a tiny, meek creature, but its effect was deadly. I was having one of those Edenic mornings in our backyard, enjoying the birdsong and the sound of water cascading down the fountain wall. I remember thinking, Life does not get better than this. And then I saw him. The interloper was a little gray mouse, staring down from a wire atop an aviary. I didn't know enough about rodents to realize that they are normally nocturnal. If you see one during the day, there is probably an overpopulation of them running around at night. The mouse trembled at the sight of me, then ran off toward our neighbor's yard. I put any thought of poison or trapping out of my head. What harm could a little mouse do?

A lot. The Australian crested doves' offspring were the first; then the adults succumbed. All fourteen birds were dead in a few weeks' time. My stomach churned every morning when I went out to the Annex Aviary, where they were housed. I was afraid of what I would find. What was killing them? I called Dr. Varner and we went over every aspect of my bird husbandry. No, I hadn't changed food, brought in new food, or sprayed anything with insecticide or another poison. Then she asked, "Having any trouble with rats or mice?"

It suddenly dawned on me that for the past week, I'd seen something odd in one of the feeding dishes in the Annex. I wasn't sure exactly where the little black flakes had come from. I thought that maybe the manufacturer had changed the formula and added a new type of seed. Then I made the connection: That cute little mouse. Rodent excrement contains bacteria that are deadly to birds. There was so much of it inside the Annex that I suspected there was a lot more than one mouse running around.

Dr. Varner came to look at the aviaries and suggested ways I could address the problem. She insisted that I renovate the Annex right away. Gone was a fountain I'd had built. Gone was the natural floor made up of grasses, pebbles, and sand. I installed concrete flooring. It was ugly, but it was now possible to clean it by hosing down the surface. I hired an exterminator and fully rodent-proofed each enclosure. Finally things were stabilized. But I was left with some nagging doubts.

Of course, I had called the Browns when my birds started dying. They suggested putting antibiotics in the water so that all the birds could be treated as a preventive measure. Dr. Varner didn't agree. She insisted that I wait until a bird showed signs of illness and then remove the bird from the flock and treat it individually. Her reason was that antibiotics in water are impossible to dose accurately. Some birds might ingest too much while others got too little. I followed her advice and didn't treat the birds until they were symptomatic, but by then it was too late; the sick birds died, and even more had been exposed. By the time the epidemic had run its course, I had lost thirty-three birds.

I had great admiration for Dr. Varner and I was grateful for all that she had done for my birds, but I realized that there is a limit to veterinary knowledge about birds. Those who breed and live with birds have a practical, hands-on knowledge that draws much from experience and intuition. At times it seems as though breeders and veterinarians are working at cross-purposes. I've seen mistrust and skepticism on both sides.

The breeders feel that vets charge a lot of money for too few viable solutions. Louis and Carol used to send their dead birds off to a well-known vet school so that necropsies could be done and the cause of death identified. At Pandemonium, we do that regularly, even though Carol had told me, "We spent a fortune but rarely got answers." Many of the avian vets that I've met have little respect for bird breeders, complaining that they often don't seek professional treatment for their birds and rely instead on medicines ordered from catalogs.

I'd love to see more collaboration between vets and breeders. From my perspective, the best bird care would combine the science of veterinary medicine with the experience of breeders. I've also become passionate about trying to preserve the accumulated knowledge of breeders. Since the old-time breeders rarely wrote anything down and apprentices are no longer common, a breeder's knowledge dies with him. If there were more documentation, all of us, including vets, could better take advantage of what breeders have learned through trial and error.

Louis and Carol were extremely supportive during the epidemic of illness and death brought by the mice. They took turns telling me stories about times they'd screwed up. They listened patiently when I'd burst into tears discussing the loss. They'd been there. They had compassion, but they also had a broader outlook. Birds died all the time, they cautioned. And sometimes you had to do the unthinkable for the good of the flock.

There is a terrible story about a bird epidemic that I heard at one of the Browns' parties. Whether it's apocryphal I can't say, because Chet, the man at the center of the tale, died a few years ago. He was an experienced breeder in the San Diego area. The incident took place during an outbreak of exotic Newcastle disease, a virulent, always fatal virus that mainly affects confined poultry. In the 2002–3 epidemic that hit Southern California and other parts of the Southwest, 3.16 million birds either died of the disease or were ordered destroyed by a government task force. Exotic Newcastle is most communicable in crowded environments like poultry farms. Chickens are the most vulnerable. Given the disease's devastating toll, the official policy was scorched earth: Kill them all.

Chet felt that his exotic species—isolated in their aviaries, far from affected poultry farms—were fine. There was no sign of sickness and no outside contact. So when a team of inspectors arrived with kill orders for the generations of exotic birds he had raised and loved over many years, Chet met them with a shotgun. He didn't threaten the men but explained his position. His birds were healthy and didn't need to die. The inspectors were adamant: Destroy them.

Chet wheeled and turned the gun on a group of his birds. Each blast tore apart beautiful creatures he loved. The aviary became a hideous abattoir of feathers, blood, and screams. Chet was aiming at his fourth or fifth bird when the inspectors turned and retreated—for good. Either the man was crazy and dangerous or he was following their orders. They weren't sticking around to find out which.

Chet saved the rest of his flock with that dreadful execution of a few. I was hardly prepared when I was faced with a "kill" decision on a much smaller scale. The enemy was also unseen but deadly. And it had been living among us for months.

The trouble began, I'm sure, with a pair of olive pigeons. I had noticed that they weren't moving around much. I thought they needed a change of habitat, so I moved them to one of the sunlit back aviaries. The olive male seemed to have something on his wing, but he kept his distance and I couldn't get a close look. Then the olive female died.

I was getting tougher after that first round of fatalities. I wanted to learn how to do a necropsy, so I took the bird's body to Louis, who had promised to teach me how to look for the cause of death. I learned some necropsy skills, but we couldn't determine what had killed the pigeon. Louis thought it might have been complications from a burst egg, which would prove to be wrong. Then the male died, and the vet identified a growth on his wing as a manifestation of a mycobacterium. This could be devastating to all the birds that shared the aviary.

Sure enough, we had another bird down soon after—a Guinea turaco could not fly. I had a special feeling for this gallant male, who had saved two of his babies after their mother died. He fed them, day and night, by himself. I moved him to an isolation cage and gave him antibiotics, and he started to improve. But the results from a biopsy done by the vet showed that he had an untreatable strain of the mycobacterium. It was probably the same strain, I now realized, that had killed the olive pigeons. It was vital that we know for sure, the vet insisted. By then, I knew too well what that meant.

The disease would have to be speciated—identified—by a necropsy of a bird known to have it. If we hoped to find the proper treatment to save the other birds, we would have to euthanize the turaco and send his tissues to a lab to identify the mycobacterium strain. I made the decision, but I had someone else take the doomed turaco to the vet. In the end, two labs were unable to identify the strain. If there were any treatment, finding it would be nearly impossible.

I asked several avian vets what I could do to protect the other birds from the spread of the disease. The answer was unanimous and devastating: Kill all the birds that have been exposed. For us, that would mean killing 90 percent of our birds, including the crowned pigeons and the green-napeds. It would all but wipe us out and further stress the populations of the rare species we breed.

I was obsessed with finding a solution. The severity of the problem and the ticking clock left me frantic and sleep-deprived—not a useful combination. The family was sputtering along on autopilot when I suddenly realized that my best resource was right there at home. Tom is a pulmonologist and no stranger to treatment options for respiratory infections in humans. I asked for his help, and he consulted with some avian vets. Together they devised a drug regimen for the birds. But before we could try it, I had to identify which birds might be ill and determine how we would administer the medicine. An alliance emerged: A neighborhood pharmacist canvassed his professional association to help devise the best method of drug delivery. A breeder referred us to an out-of-state lab that would do testing for the disease for a very reasonable price. Volunteers helped net birds so that they could be tested.

Thanks to our circle of experts, we had developed a protocol that seemed effective. The birds that tested positive were treated for fourteen months. Every time we retested, the results came up negative. Finally, recovery was under way. I won't say I relaxed, but I had a little time to think.

I took a hard look back at the gains and losses of this crisis period—the carpenter Ron's misdeeds, the rodent-borne illness, and the mycobacterium—and realized that I didn't have to try to figure everything out by myself. In the collaborative effort to save Pandemonium's diverse flock, I found a community of like-minded people who are passionate about birds and active in leadership roles in bird research and conservation. And as the horror of Ron's transgressions receded, and so many people came forward to help us in our time of need, I found a renewed faith in our own species.

I also had a lot of bills. Four days for a single bird's stay at a veterinary clinic could run to almost a thousand dollars. I had found a facility to do necropsies for free, but keeping birds fed and healthy was also becoming wildly expensive. We were buying seed by the pallet—and the ton. A local big-box store had been donating unsold fruit, but it wasn't enough. The feeding bowls that go out to our avian fruit eaters every morning look as if they could easily be part of a four-star hotel's brunch buffet: blueberries, pomegranate seeds, cantaloupe, papaya. An entire second refrigerator in our kitchen is filled with the upscale produce at all times. The family was not enthusiastic when I decided to save money by growing our own worms in the garage.

I tried to be diligent in keeping records of the birds' health as well as what I spent on them. Always, I'd vow to economize. I had a sign made for what I swore was the Last Aviary; soon there were the Next to the Last Aviary and the Last Last Aviary. But needs grew faster still. There were more calls from people who had lost their homes to foreclosure or were ill. The phone kept ringing: please, take my bird. Something had to change—and fast.

# THIRTEEN

# Let's Get Serious

Neighbors often drop in to visit our birds. At one time we also welcomed strangers—passersby, bicyclists, hikers headed to the nature trail across the street—who wandered up our driveway past Pandemonium's inconspicuous mosaic sign. Now that we breed rare birds, we need to give our birds privacy, so we are closed to all visitors other than friends. In the early years, more often than not they were drawn by the brash, trumpeting honk of our two East African cranes. Ferguson is the default town crier and self-appointed gatekeeper, but Olivia can summon a mighty wind as well. Their towering aviary is near the Pandemonium entryway, with a giant gold Buddha at its center. Both cranes like to perch high on a ledge, where they dance, preen, and posture to the delight of the gawking, flightless souls walking on our path or on the street below. If Amadeus is our front-door welcome bird, the cranes are our yard greeters. They often float down to the ground to say hello to visitors at the front of their enclosure.

Coming face-to-face with such extraordinary creatures is an unexpected thrill for just about anyone.

One day in 2009, a stranger rang the doorbell and asked
if it was okay to look at the cranes. He introduced himself as
Ben and said he had just returned from a tour of Africa, where
he had seen cranes in the wild. He'd heard about Pandemonium and wanted to visit our cranes. I decided to walk out with
him and take him through the long way, to see some other birds
and the grounds. Ben was amazed when we walked through
the gate.

"I had no *idea* . . ."

I'd heard that before.

It was an eyeful. As we walked along the paths, everything
was abloom: gardenias, acacia, geraniums, flowering hedges and
herbs. Annuals spilled out of pots and mosaic troughs; eucalyptus and manzanita branches and live shrubs greened the aviaries' interiors. Food and water dishes for the birds are made of
brightly glazed pottery, heavy enough to withstand tipping by
impatient diners. Along the stone-and-pebble paths, we have
planted bird- and butterfly-friendly plants like buddleia (butterfly bush), raspberries, blueberries, blackberries, lantana, and
salvia for our wild avian visitors. Benches to sit on and observe
birds dot the landscape.

The path to the cranes' big aviary passes through a courtyard
that houses the parrots and macaws. Those companion-bird
aviaries are equipped with enough enrichment toys to stock a

preschool; the big cage marked TICO'S TERRITORY is hung with rope pulls, bright wood blocks, bells, and, of course, a dummy lock or two to pick. There is art everywhere: statuary, mosaic birdbaths, sculptures and decorative lattices bolted to aviary walls. Found objects from yard sales, donations, or the flea market—from funky watering cans to a gaily painted Costa Rican donkey cart—have been repurposed as planters. Inside and outside the Saint Francis Aviary, there are half a dozen likenesses of that venerated animal lover from Assisi who is most often depicted with birds on his shoulders and arms. Even workstation sinks, gates, and doors have some mosaic flourishes, thanks to a talented and prolific local artist who can't seem to stay away. She says she finds inspiration here.

Add the rainbow flash of exotic wings, and it's a lovely place to be. Pandemonium is a very happy village most of the time. Sometimes I'm apt to forget this as I fuss over a loose hinge or a lethargic-looking pigeon. That day, Ben was a quiet and patient listener as I voiced my frustrations over maintaining so many birds, the work involved, and the financial burden. I must have been especially tired. I wasn't complaining so much as trying to figure out how to do a better job of caring for everybody. It turned out that Ben himself ran a foundation and knew a great deal about nonprofit organizations.

He turned from watching Ferguson's long-legged clowning and asked me, "What's your vision, Michele? And what are your fears?"

Wow. I didn't have ready answers for him. Ben suggested I take some time to write down my dreams for Pandemonium and list the anxieties and obstacles that might stand in their way. That evening, once all the birds were settled for the night, I sat down in my office and thought about our conversation. Pandemonium had been changing, but it had happened so slowly and organically that I'd hardly noticed. I realized that we had most of what it took to be a nonprofit organization—a mission, goals, an established facility, breeding programs. I was also up to speed on the required record keeping, since we already kept track of bird health and statistics as well as expenses.

One thing was starkly apparent. The operating expenses had become a large financial burden that our family budget could no longer support. Outside funding was a must if we were to keep going in the best way possible for the birds. We were already a nonprofit organization in every respect except for official designation. I had simply been too busy with the day-to-day operations to look very far ahead. It took a perfect stranger like Ben to nudge me toward the next logical phase.

He was right about step one. Before I moved ahead with any plan to formalize our nonprofit status, I had to face my fears—no easy task. I had a long list of them: the financial toll my passion had taken, the worries of feeling inadequate to the growing tasks, the frustrations of a family that was getting less and less of my attention. I knew that I needed to plot a course that would better serve my multispecies family. Still, I was so thoroughly and gloriously immersed that I was afraid for any of it to change.

I was fiercely possessive about those daily joys, afraid of "success" and the loss of intimacy it might bring. As it was, I knew every bird, and every feather on that bird. I would have to surrender ownership of so much of what I considered "mine." Any founder of a nonprofit will tell you it's hard to let go. You must bring in a board that can guide you—and overrule you. You must learn to ask for money—skillfully and often. You need to take on staff—even if it's all volunteer, as ours is—to handle the greater administrative and public awareness tasks that a functional nonprofit demands.

Finally, though, I took the plunge. Pandemonium Aviaries would become a legally designated not-for-profit. That meant shifting our grassroots start-up to an exacting business model that met government standards for operations and accounting. It seemed daunting, but I reminded myself that my graduate degree in business and my work experience counted for plenty. Hadn't I guided Silicon Valley start-ups? Having been active on a humane-society board, wasn't I prepared for the ethical and economic debates, the crafting of mission statements and fund-raising goals?

We applied for status as a 501(c)(3) not-for-profit and got the designation in April 2010, retroactive to November 2009. By then we were ready. The facility itself had already undergone upgrades for no other reason than to better care for the birds.

Following that awful epidemic with the rodent-borne virus and then the mycobacterium, we stopped all transferring of birds between aviaries. We made sure that the companion birds never came into contact with the wild species. We excavated and removed all the substrate in areas where birds had become sick. A crew in hazmat gear—suits, helmets, respirators—blow-torched aviary floors and installed basins of disinfectant and rubber flip-flops for use by anyone entering an aviary. We continued our practice of testing for parasites and diseases carefully and often. At this point I assumed our birds were healthier than any wild birds in the area.

Though it wasn't requisite, I also decided to subject our facility to tough professional scrutiny so that it would qualify for the Model Aviculture Program (MAP). That voluntary program certifies aviculturists' operations through inspections by veterinarians in order to improve avian health and husbandry. The MAP guidelines also encourage accurate record keeping on exotic birds to improve the productivity and offspring of breeding pairs. We did it all, from wiring to water delivery, heat lamps, and disinfectant procedures. Pandemonium passed with flying colors.

What I could not keep at bay with netting and disinfectant were those messy affairs of the heart. From the start, I had always declared our sanctuary "birdcentric." In other words, when we have to choose between the needs of humans and birds, the birds win. There was a corollary that would probably be challenged when I gave up sole control of decision making. I had begun with the premise that all our rescue birds were equal—from Sweetie, the two-dollar quail, to the rare GNPP Gwen. Both had needed expensive surgery. Both got it.

What was fair? Wise? Justifiable? I still had a stubborn habit of expending time, money, and energy on those I probably could not save—a vulnerability that would have to change if we were to move forward as a viable sanctuary. It was time to start thinking in terms of the "greatest good." By 2009, Pandemonium was sanctuary to more than 250 birds, most of them rescued and thriving. Our population was still growing, but the number of hours in a day had stayed the same. Nonprofit status would allow us to recruit and train volunteers to absorb some of the workload. But would I trust them?

At a time when my internal debate over such matters was getting pretty loud and feisty, along came tiny Ella.

The aviary that housed Oscar and the rest of our Lady Gouldian finches was a very busy place—and I'd held off going in until a new brother-and-sister pair had fledged. Finally I had to go in to clean. When I moved the green-gray baby finch, it showed a normal fear response, trying to avoid my hands. His yellow-hued sister didn't react at all. I waved my hands and fingers at her. No reaction. She was blind.

A wonderful vet named Rose Franklin had replaced Anne Calloway, who had moved north to the Seattle area. Rose agreed to come have a look at our blind baby. A friend suggested I name her Ella Finchgerald, as Ella Fitzgerald was also sight impaired. Rose pronounced the finch normal except for her vision, and though she wasn't optimistic, she suggested we try antibiotic eye drops and weigh the bird daily to make sure she was eating and gaining weight. I was willing. Of course I was.

I covered the aviary floor with a crazy quilt of different surface materials—carpet squares, bamboo flooring squares, children's rubber alphabet play mats—interspersed so that Ella could feel her way around. As I worked, I always knew where she was because of the racket. Ella had so many needs that she cheeped ceaselessly. To get her to drink, I gently dunked her head in a small water dish—one of four, each placed in a corner. I set up a bed made of a plastic food dish lined with soft paper so that in the evening, when the other finches flew up to their perches, I could place her safely in bed. I didn't want her to sleep on the floor.

Soon her brother had begun eating on his own; Ella's parents were still feeding her, and I was still leading her to water. I scattered seed on the ground along the way so that Ella would walk on it and find it. I put soaked seed on her beak. Around the sanctuary, a few eyebrows were raised at the time spent fussing over a tiny finch that was most likely doomed; I was in there for hours but felt I had to be. I was aghast when I saw an older finch peck Ella on the head—possibly fed up with her racket. But Ella cheeped on. One day, I watched her brother spend an inordinate amount of time feeding at a millet spray. He then walked up to Ella and fed her. Later in the day, he begged food from his parents and flew down to feed his sister again. What a guy!

The day came when the adults stopped feeding Ella. Her brother persisted, but he wasn't very adept at connecting with Ella's open beak. I did what I could. Finally Ella realized that food and water could be found in dishes, and she bumbled toward them. I also noticed that she would spend much of her day cheeping at the aviary gate. Then I realized: when Ella heard the creak of the gate, she knew it was me—the one who gave her water, scattered the seed, brought her up from the cold into the cozy night nest. She was calling me; how could I walk on by?

By then, Pandemonium supporters were following my e-mail updates on Ella and rooting for the little finch. A month after Ella and her brother had hatched, I found myself typing a final dispatch: "I'm very sorry to tell you that Ella died sometime last night." I had found her on the floor. It was the first time she had climbed out of her bed at night. The weather had been hot that day and she may have needed to find water. We'll never know.

I took some flak for trying so hard to keep a profoundly handicapped bird alive, and maybe some of it was deserved. I thought a lot about readjusting the ratio of emotion and intellect. Since that time, my actions have changed—not because of the increase in the number of birds, but because of the non-profit status. I have to answer to others for my actions now, and to consult more people. I'm comfortable making decisions that are best for the organization, even if they aren't optimal for me. Would I have sold some birds born and raised here in order to purchase the breeding Nicobars pigeons we needed? No. But for the species and the organization, it was the right thing to do.

I had to stop the foster care program, and soon after, I ceased accepting rescue birds. There's nothing as costly as a free bird. I've certainly found that true, even though a bird—unwanted by someone else—can turn out to be the key to your future. And though I didn't know it, the catalyst to a huge change in our operation was pecking desultorily in a back aviary—a shy, somewhat aloof giveaway that had been with us for years.

# FOURTEEN

# Blessed Events

I was cleaning the Victoria crowned pigeons' aviary. Again. That chore can be time consuming because they always want to socialize. They bob their tails like puppies in greeting, brush up against my legs, and step in their food bowls as I'm trying to work. Their clumsy attentions are flattering and frustrating in equal measure. Coffee is still the most effusive greeter, often in the company of his new mate, Tia. They had settled in together nicely—I had been able to find Coffee's sister, Wing, a mate named Mike—but I didn't realize how close they had become. Once Coffee had finished his welcoming ritual, I noticed that there was an egg in the nest box. It was clear that Coffee and Tia had scant interest in their egg, because they were no longer sitting in the nest.

A few years before, I would not have been so distressed by the discovery. But since we had adopted and refined a strategic breeding program, a "wasted" egg—leaving an unattended egg for too long impairs or destroys its viability—was another reminder that time was running out for these birds. By 2010 we had begun practicing conservation breeding in earnest with five imperiled species: the GNPPs, bleeding-heart doves, Nicobar pigeons, Victoria crowned pigeons, and their very close cousins, blue crowned pigeons. We expanded our programs, invited help from a multidisciplinary team of experts, and put in place an internal structure to support ambitious goals.

Carefully I examined the abandoned egg closely for any cracks or signs of decay. Like the GNPPs and other birds from island habitats, Victoria crowned pigeons do not lay large clutches of eggs. In the slower pattern of island reproduction, they lay just one egg at a time, which they incubate for one month. If the egg hatches, the baby will not leave the nest for at least a month, and the parents continue to feed that baby for three or four more months beyond that.

A large number of eggs laid by crowned pigeons in captivity never hatch for a variety of reasons. At Pandemonium, the main problem was that our birds were too tame. Coffee and Tia got off their nest box in order to socialize with me. Sometimes they decided they'd rather stroll around than return to the nest. I held the egg in my hand and starting thinking . . . what if? What did I have to lose by sticking it in the incubator that shared space with the more conventional appliances in our kitchen?

At the time, I was busy training a new set of volunteers. I forgot about the egg until a few days later. After all, I wasn't expecting anything. I decided to look at the egg inside the incubator. By holding a bright light next to the egg, or candling, I was able to see the forming baby and air cell inside. These were good signs. Three weeks later, I found a telltale pinprick on the outside of the shell. The chick was attempting to break out.

This could be incredible—a baby Victoria crowned pigeon born at Pandemonium! I hardly dared let myself hope. Then right away, I saw a problem. The baby seemed to be pecking an irregular pattern of pinpricks that could fail to open the egg. What to do? As I pondered some sort of intervention, I talked to the egg. The baby inside responded with peeping noises and a good deal of movement. It was my low-tech version of the fetal stress tests that monitor human babies in utero. This little guy was likely in some distress, given the pecking pattern, but I knew that it was best not to take the baby out of the shell.

Hatching is something a bird should do on its own. A baby bird's emergence from a neatly cracked egg is just one tiny moment in a complex process of developmental sequences. The baby must be able to move and breathe inside the shell, crack the shell open with precision, and then break out and free itself with instinctive movements that trigger more physiological responses it will need to survive outside the shell. Many baby birds die before, during, or even after hatching because some fragile link in the developmental sequence goes awry.

I knew that a huge struggle would soon begin inside the shell. Just before hatching, the baby would move around in a way that sealed the blood vessels on the inside perimeter of the shell. It was a critical period that could take a couple of days. Even in the wild, survival is hardly a given; eggs and baby birds often die as the result of disease, predators, or other bad luck. But when you're breeding birds, especially rare or endangered birds, uncertainty isn't good enough if there is anyone who might have useful information to improve the odds of survival. I had been making rounds of phone calls to top breeders across the country for help as the egg incubated. Luckily, despite the secretive nature of breeders, a couple were willing to share information, but there was always a caveat.

"I really can't say for sure."

"There's just no telling."

"You know the odds on these birds, Michele."

I did get some disturbing information: even if we managed a successful hatching, it was not unusual to have the babies die within the fourth or twelfth week. No one knew why, and the mystery would most likely persist because of that enduring lack of cooperation between the breeders on the one hand, and the scientists and vets on the other. Communication was almost nonexistent. The breeders possessed most of the hands-on knowledge about raising exotic bird babies, but save for a few exceptions like Louis and Carol, they just weren't going to pass it on. Call it snobbery, call it stubbornness—it still makes me crazy, when there is so much to be gained by pooling information.

I had to face facts. The rare baby in the egg was pretty much on its own—and so was I. I hovered, I fretted, and I was very anxious when we all had to pile into the car and head to Tom's cousin's house for Thanksgiving dinner. When we returned, I ran to the incubator. Nothing yet. I was too nervous to sleep, so I settled into my office nearby for the night. I decided to stay up with some paperwork. That would be a lot better than standing in front of the incubator, straining my eyes for signs of movement within the egg. As I shut off the lights in the kitchen to leave the room, I wondered if the baby needed darkness, as it would have in the nest. Or maybe it needed some circadian cycle of day and night. I just didn't know. I checked the incubator often that night—and of course, I missed the hatch. But there was our Victoria crowned baby outside the broken shell—naked and plug-ugly. Now what? Without his parents' feathered warmth and a nest, the chick had only featherless humans.

For both Tom and me, it was love at first sight. The depth of Tom's reaction amazed me. After all these years and all these birds, for the first time he had fallen hard for a baby bird. He named him Peep because "every time I walk by, he peeps at me."

I called Carol right away with the news. She was thrilled but cautious. She reminded me to leave the baby alone, and instructed, "You're not to feed him until you see a little poop." Peep complied, and the regimen began. In the weeks ahead, whenever Tom was at home, he was hand-feeding Peep a commercially prepared baby-bird formula or just hanging out with him. The two sometimes just sat peacefully, Peep snuggled on the warm chest, his head tucked under Tom's chin. Sometimes I'd find them both passed out in front of the TV.

Tom's medical training kicked in. He charted Peep's growth curve daily and posted feeding instructions—five pages, single spaced—on the cabinet above Peep's box. When he was at home, he took over Peep's care. Unlike baby parrots, whose parents insert their beaks into the baby's crop to provide nutrition, baby pigeons suck regurgitated food in from their parents. Peep drank from a tiny shot glass—Carol's preferred vessel.

Hand-feeding is grueling; it takes intense concentration every two hours, day and night. The process is also bonding. You become so attuned to the baby's needs, so sensitized to the tiniest changes and nuances, that it's a bit of an interspecies mind meld. Nevertheless, no matter how much we cared, we couldn't be good or even adequate parents to Peep. A bird parent knows when and how to feed its baby, when to warm it in the nest, and when to step away and insist that the baby start to feed itself. With exotic birds like Peep, it takes trial and error as well as scrupulous record keeping to make the data available for others to study so that we can advance our collective understanding. Every hatchling matters because the survival clock is ticking.

Tom fed Peep for seven weeks. Then we brought in another Victoria crowned, one with a maternal personality, to teach Peep how to find and pick up food and eat it. One day in his second month of life, Peep seemed ill with some sort of respiratory problem. I raced Peep to an avian vet with a national reputation, a sort of celebrity vet, whom I hadn't used before. Peep was on his feet when I left him there, but the following day I arrived to find him lying in an oxygen chamber, extremely ill. We were right up against that twelve-week danger period I'd been warned about. As I looked at Peep, alone in the oxygen chamber and struggling, I wondered if I ever should have moved him. Maybe the change in environment and different handlers had been too much of a shock. Peep died on January 25— Tom's birthday.

We were very sad, of course. But I pulled myself together and acted like a conservation breeder. I ordered a necropsy; it showed nothing. We later bought an oxygen tank for Pandemonium so that I'd never have to be separated from an ailing rare baby again. I'm convinced now that it was a mistake taking Peep far away; he might have died anyway, but nobody can keep a vigil better and with a closer eye than a pair of doting parents, albeit human stand-ins.

SIX YEARS AFTER that first pair of green-naped pheasant pigeons arrived mysteriously by mail, I still had hopes for breeding those inscrutable birds. Though they were not officially listed as endangered, virtually none had been seen in recent years in New Guinea, and their distinctive call had seldom been heard. The lack of information on their habits was frustrating. I tried varying their habitat, moving them around to different aviaries in the hopes that one of them would provide the right mix of space, light, greenery, and privacy for them to raise a baby. Like Victoria crowneds, GNPPs lay a single egg that they incubate for a month. Unless they feel comfortable in an aviary, they don't even attempt to nest. Finally I had an aviary built just for them in one of the few private areas left in our backyard.

Once the birds were settled, finding the right nest box became the next challenge. Not a single bird keeper that I consulted had ever raised a GNPP, and most declined to offer suggestions on what to try. One breeder told me that he had heard it was necessary to provide a loosely woven platform about three feet off the ground. I didn't know how to weave one, but I was determined to try.

First, I tried grass hay. I carried it into the aviary in an old weather-beaten wooden fruit box. Years earlier, I had found it in the crook of a tree, abandoned after a long-ago harvest. The pear and apple farms were gone before our neighborhood was developed. The box was a sort only found in antique shops or flea markets these days. In the midst of constructing the ledge to hold the woven platform, I was called away. I left the hay-filled box on its side. When I returned the next day to resume building, the green-napeds had already claimed the box as their nesting site.

An old fruit box is now the standard nest box for the GNPPs. They will use only a fruit box that is completely solid and has the original wood. Attach new wood slats to fix a broken old box, and the birds will reject it. The ledge it sits on is also important. I never did figure out how to construct a ledge that was not solid, yet was strong enough to support birds and the fruit box. I suspect that the breeder's suggestion for a woven platform had more to do with the GNPP's infamous startle response than with nesting. If one were startled on the ground below the nest and jumped straight up, impact with a solid wood ledge might kill the bird by breaking its neck or back.

Weaving a platform proved impossible, so I positioned solid wooden ledges just right—not so high that the birds would refuse it, but not so low as to present a danger to a frightened bird below. Nothing about keeping these birds is easy. I had to move slowly around them in the aviary and keep my distance because they are so fearful of people. Lancelot, one of our original pair, was pretty relaxed around me, but the newer pair in our GNPP flock seemed happier if left to themselves.

Despite their acceptance of the fruit box nest, nothing much was succeeding within. It wasn't for lack of trying. We had nine failures, some parent-incubated in the nest, and some with eggs I'd tried to incubate. Then, late in 2011, I found an abandoned egg. It was a forlorn sight. I was beginning to fear that the birds had finally given up. I might have thrown in the towel as well were it not for another of those mysterious "aha" moments born of coincidence.

One morning I had been reading some literature on GNPPs that I had finally been able to dig up. I learned that babies hatched in the wild were born during the rainiest season—in the rain forest. I thought about it: our weather was so much drier that humidity levels must be inadequate for the formation of a healthy, viable eggshell. I was pondering this later that day when I had a phone call from an exultant zookeeper. One of the first GNPP babies hatched in a decade had just been born at his zoo. The zoo's GNPP parents had chosen a small rock ledge near a waterfall as their nesting site. Bingo! With that information and what I'd read earlier, I was convinced that low humidity was the reason for our birds' many failures. With a sinking heart, I took a hard look at the greenhouse that held my beloved orchids, the result of thirty years' collecting and propagating. Tending them had been a joy. As the collection grew, I had installed an automatic misting system—just the thing for our rain forest nesters.

Out went the orchids—given away, for the most part, though a few favorites still "board" in a local orchid grower's vast greenhouse. I rationalized my loss. Tending the plants weekly had become too much of a luxury, given the birds' demands at that point. In went the GNPPs. And on went the misting system, especially during very dry spells. When the birds were nesting again, I kept track of the temperature and rainfall and adjusted the greenhouse humidity carefully.

I had vowed not to check on the sitting birds too often, but I couldn't contain my curiosity. I wouldn't go into the aviary; I'd just take a quick peek from outside. At the very least, I hoped to see a broken eggshell on the ground, which would tell me whether the egg had hatched. There was no sign of an empty shell or a baby, and it was well past time. I was terribly disappointed, but I felt worse for the birds—until I saw her. The ungainly little baby had been in the nest box, as quiet and shy as her parents. The secretive GNPPs had actually hidden the broken eggshell under some bedding on the nesting shelf— perhaps an instinctive behavior to avoid tipping predators to the presence of a tasty young fledgling.

I'll admit it. I loved making the phone call.

"Louis! We did it! We have a green-naped baby. And she's fine!"

Her parents took excellent care of her, and the baby thrived. We named her Mitzi.

SHE WAS A quiet little bird, but her arrival made considerable noise in aviculture circles. Then a second GNPP baby arrived. We named her Peka, after a river in Papua New Guinea. Overall, 2011–12 was a year of amazing gains for Pandemonium's conservation mission. We had overseen live births of two rare species that most zoos and the best private breeders couldn't manage, and with very minimal resources. As a relatively new nonprofit, we had some measurable results to show potential donors. Our website crowed the new baby news—and our mission statement called for greater conservation efforts. With Pandemonium's enhanced profile, our first big fund raiser—a garden and aviary tour we called the Victoria Crown Affair—was a great success.

For me, still spattered with bird poop and piloting my pickup to haul ever more seed, those first successful births brought a bit of sweet validation. I was being taken seriously by zoo aviculturists; once-dismissive breeders were now calling me when they were looking for birds and advice. We have opened our aviaries to visiting zoo officials, aviculture societies, educators, and breeders. I also share what I have learned as the conservation columnist for the Avicultural Society of America's bulletin and as a speaker at professional conferences.

The small, private moments, though, still hold the most satisfaction. The best times are the mornings, when it's just me and the birds. A year after Mitzi's hatching, I found myself sneaking around outside the greenhouse once again. I suspect I'll always be nervous and impatient when awaiting new life. I rubbed a spot on the dusty window to see the nest box within.

Mitzi, hale and hearty, was going to be a mom. Our GNPP flock has gone from two to eighteen—the largest in the world.

I know it's way too soon for celebration; there is so much that can and probably will go wrong. But I am also coming to realize that in our efforts to understand birds and partner with them, meaningful advances don't necessarily come in big leaps. As I learned from Oscar the finch when we built the ladder, no matter how high the aspirations, progress comes in incremental steps. Yes, bird by bird.

EPILOGUE

I may have been trembling just a bit as the stagehand adjusted my wireless mike. I peered out beyond the lights and saw rows of expectant young faces filling the auditorium at the Castilleja School in Palo Alto. Just offstage, Fanny, one of our Victoria crowned pigeons, sat calmly in her cage, awaiting her star turn.

I was about to deliver a TEDx talk, a version of the live conference and Internet-streamed TED talks in technology, entertainment, and design (hence TED) dedicated to "ideas worth spreading." Addressing a potentially global audience— my talk would be on the website—was a long, long way from cradling that injured dove on the highway.

How would I get my backyard odyssey into the six-minute limit? What message did I want to give this audience, which included a lot of kids? Did I dare tell them my most outrageous dream? It's so crucial to impress upon the planet's next stewards the scope and urgency of conservation. Education is one of the key platforms in Pandemonium's mission statement. Yet when I had approached many elementary and middle schools in the San Francisco Peninsula offering a free enrichment program on endangered species—complete with exotic live birds like Fanny—not a single principal accepted, though some seemed regretful. The most common excuse: We're so busy "teaching to the test" that we have no time. Wish we did. Thanks anyhow.

What luck to be reaching out to young people and others, in a format they were receptive to: a birdcentric download! The talks are videotaped before a live audience. When the red lights blinked atop the cameras, I began: "Today I'm going to talk to you about saving animals. . . . Who was the world's first conservationist?"

I recapped the story of Noah and his species-saving ark. "Noah," I told them, "has no animal-saving skills. . . . Nowhere does it say he even likes animals. But he's a good person. He does it because it's the right thing to do."

And the purpose of an ark? It's like other boats in appearance and in the materials used to build it. The difference between an ark and other boats is its function. Other boats are designed to take you safely to someplace new. The purpose of an ark? It's to keep you safe while the world around you becomes new.

Noah's biblical world was transformed by a flood. Our present-day ecological changes are the inventions of man. I clicked the slide projector to show a sixteenth-century rendering of an odd-looking bird and asked the students to consider the dodo, rendered extinct in just eighty years after the boats of Portuguese colonists landed on Mauritius. Dodoes were hunted and forced from their habitat by the incursion of palm oil plantations, which destroyed the forests.

Suddenly there was a collective intake of breath, a chorus of oohs. Owing to a slight miscue, the stagehands had wheeled Fanny onstage a bit prematurely. The sight of that strange, beautiful blue creature always startles people. When things quieted down, I went on to relate the sad parallel fate of the Victoria crowned pigeon: now the world's largest pigeon, more hunting, more palm oil plantations, more habitat destruction . . .

"Sound familiar?" I asked the darkened room.

There are very few birds of Fanny's species left in captivity, I explained. Pandemonium has the second-largest flock in the world. But there is no comprehensive program—yet—to try to save them. I told the students about the Louis Browns of the bird world, knowledgeable types who are pretty endangered as well: "These birds are in the hands of a small group of breeders. They're old, and when they die, the birds are sold at auction or given to friends and they're effectively lost. What's also tragic is that the knowledge these breeders have accumulated over their lifetimes is also lost."

I told them the story of Pandemonium. I clicked on a slide of the green-naped pheasant pigeon whose death had caused her mate to cry, and I conveyed my shock at finding out that there are only thirty-two known birds of his kind left in all the world's zoos.

"I discovered that once-common birds were going extinct in the wild," I said. "They were rare in captivity. And without my realizing it, my backyard had become an ark."

I wasn't claiming biblical import; I used the ark analogy to convey the oceans of problems and the tough odds facing our little operation. I explained our change in direction from a one-to-one rescue group to a nonprofit with the global mission to save lots of birds from extinction. I rolled out my dream: Pandemonium has a conservation plan called ARC—Avian Recovery for Conservation—that just might save the birds and the knowledge to raise more of them. If, that is, we can raise the money to fund it. We want to save the aviculture secrets before the master breeders die, before the birds are dispersed.

"We will set up little arks," I said, adding that we're looking at land and locations in different parts of the country. We'll buy the flocks before they're dispersed and let them stay with the breeders, have apprentices learn what they do, and then document it. When the breeders pass on, the birds will go into conservancy in ARC facilities.

By the time I finished outlining my hopes beyond Pandemonium, my time was up. I asked the audience a final question: "If you lived in the sixteen hundreds and had the chance, would you have saved the dodo?"

I drove home with Fanny, feeling pretty good. The bird was dozing after her resplendent performance. My mind shifted back to the purely practical: another load of seed to pick up, a new intern to train, and then some research about our homegrown mealworms, which seemed to be escaping from their box no matter what I used. Ah, the glamorous life. There was also a volunteer meeting about conducting a tour of Pandemonium for a summer enrichment camp for disadvantaged city children. Their counselors always ask us to invite the kids. We always have a ball.

WEEKS LATER, THE kids arrived. Three vans pulled up, and a gaggle of four-, five-, and six-year-olds tumbled out into our driveway. Their camp counselors were already on "shhhhh" patrol.

"Use your inside voices around the birds, guys!"

"Calm down, the birds are waiting for you."

The campers knew all about us from the older children who had come last summer, and from their counselors, who had been preparing them with avian-centered books and stories and a construction project. They brought us two birdhouses to hang in the redwood trees in the front yard, where gift houses from previous camp groups still held the wispy straw remnants of this spring's nests.

And so it comes and goes around in our backyard—the circle of life. the *Lion King* song by that title is a Tico-approved Disney tune. He loved to slow-dance to it with me back in the day—almost as much as he swooned for "Can You Feel the Love Tonight?" Tico, "my" special bird, may be lost to me—he only has eyes for Mylie now—and I've adjusted to that. On the morning of the tour, I only hoped he'd be on his best behavior for the children.

I had been in the kitchen when I heard the vans pull up. I was arranging a platter of bird-shaped cookies I had baked—at 4:00 a.m. I had complied with a small request from the last tour ("Add some chocolate chips? Please?"). I was tired, but I knew the visitors would be an energy boost for me and all our volunteer staff. I was also keenly aware that I was flouting Pandemonium's new "official policy" of remaining closed to the public except for special events like fund raisers and private tours for potential donors.

It's the right policy. Birds need privacy to raise their families. And for me, time spent with tour groups is time taken from the birds themselves and the mound of administrative work that our nonprofit status and conservation work now generate. But I couldn't tell these children no. It had become a tradition that we all looked forward to. It's likely that very few of these campers had computers at home to watch Pandemonium informational videos on our website, let alone a TEDx talk. And anyway, live birds are immediate, captivating, and above all a treat. Better still, they're a living, yawping lesson in ecology that won't easily slide from antsy kindergartners' or first graders' memories.

This event always takes a lot of preparation, from training volunteers to take the children around and talk about the birds to clearing out my refrigerator for the gallons of milk we'll be serving. Everyone was rushing around and a bit frazzled, and worse, the parrots were cranky. We'd had to skip dance time that morning. They don't care for disruption in their routine, and they all let me have it in their own way as I moved them, one by one, to their outdoor aviaries:

Mia Bird, the African gray parrot, looked me straight in the eye and commanded, "Focus!"

"Come here! Want out!" Shana commanded in the deep Darth Vader voice she saves for her darkest moods.

Amigo just wouldn't budge. He refused to get on my arm and muttered stormily to himself. Finally I found a stick for a perch and prodded his belly gently with it, and he grudgingly stepped up.

What was the deal with these guys? We needed them. We had cordoned off some outlying aviaries where birds were nesting. This meant the companion birds would be the main attraction for the tour. Had the kids come all the way here to get the cold shoulder from a circle of petulant psittacines? The din was growing as the camp group made its way through the center path.

Thank heaven for nosy, possessive Ferguson, the African crane. He spied the children from his high perch and spread his magnificent wings, then jumped up and down in his customary display of territorial dominance. The kids took his aggressive posturing as a grand welcome. There were squeals from below.

"He's ginormous!"

Some of the children stepped right up to the wire mesh for a better look as Ferguson flew down to inspect the interlopers. Others hung back. At ground level, the bird looked twice as tall as some of the children.

"Are you hungry? Do you want a cappuccino?" Heeeeere's Shana, not to be upstaged.

Nor will the little green guy be ignored. "Amigo, Amigo, Amigo!"

The courtyard erupted with laughter. True to their natural love of clamor, the parrots were instantly animated—all except Mylie, who perched like a prissy prom queen, awaiting adoration. Tico drew himself up to full height, then did one of his *Saturday Night Fever* moves, pulling up and extending one wing, then the other. Yo, check me out!

I'm sure my jaw dropped at his next trick. Tico, the sneakiest bird in captivity, picked his cage lock in full view of his astonished audience and pushed open the door. This was tantamount to Houdini revealing his underwater escape trick—in Times Square! More astounding: the big macaw stayed put, so that I could step right up and close the door again. Normally he would go straight into his signature escape move, then taunt me loudly and without mercy.

The Pandemonium volunteers and I exchanged astonished looks. Any outsider would think these feathered vaudevillians had rehearsed their routine for days. Prank followed prank and wisecrack until the children were breathless with laughter. As the group moved off to have a look at the plum-heads, I stopped for a wary look at Tico. The next group of children would be along in a few minutes, but having just lost his audience, he might pitch a hissy fit. His bloodcurdling screams could scare the arriving children.

But there he sat, calm and silent—a real stand-up guy. We looked at each other through the mesh, and I felt that old connection—fleetingly, but it was enough. He might well try to bite me that evening, but for the moment, my shoulders relaxed.

As the next group of children approached, Shana put the cherry on top of my morning.

"Hey, pretty mama. I love you!"

And from Tico: "Aw, shut up!"

## ACKNOWLEDGMENTS

This book would not have been possible without the vision, effort, and devotion of two remarkable people: Bonnie Solow and Amy Gash. They both went above and beyond what agent and editor normally do, and without them there would not have been a book. The birds and I are lucky you took on this project.

A special thanks to Pamela and Ed Taft, who have provided unfailing encouragement, financial support, manuscript feedback, introductions, and sage advice. Pamela and Ed, you inspire and motivate me. I am honored to have you as treasured friends and allies in the effort to save species.

Tom Raffin, Fran Scher, Alex Shubat, Dan Reddy, Uta Francke, Lynn Bahr, Diana Hawkins-Manuelian, Darlene Markovitch, Ron Haack, Flor Cuevas, Eric Helfenbein, Betsy Vobach, and Igor and Tatiana Cherkas have been on this journey with me for a long time. I am grateful to them for believing in the goal of saving birds and for their support of Pandemonium. Bridget Ferguson, Joe and Judy Passantino, Micki Regas, Virgil Bates, Carol Stanley, John Del Rio, Sheri Hanna, Sharla

Ansorge, Fern Van Saant, and Heather Riggs were instrumental in teaching me about birds and how to care for them. Brenda Kim, you were there when I needed you, listened to early chapters, and kept asking for more. And Gerri Hirshey came into my life at right time with the right help.

Michael D. Kern, our photographer, wore many hats, from management consultant to board liaison. Michael, who lives in Palo Alto and works in both the studio and the field, has been recognized worldwide for his ability to capture the simple beauty of his subjects. He has the uncanny ability to get wild animals to pose for him. It's as if they know he is there to help them.

There would not be a Pandemonium without the incredible volunteers, hard-working interns, and steadfast donors who have given time and money so generously. They have enabled our small organization to fledge and grow into an entity devoted to saving not just individual birds but whole species from half way around the world.

Then there are the birds . . . the amazing birds who ended up at Pandemonium. How can I ever thank them for letting me enter their world? They've given me the ride of a lifetime, and I'm grateful.

And, finally, there are my children, who believed that having so many animals at our home made us the "weirdest family on earth." Thank you for understanding that the animals were not rivals, that there was more than enough love to go around, and that even though we sometimes had buckets of worms in the dining room, we were weird in a good way.